Contents

✔ KU-638-207

Fit for Work?
Youth, school and (un)employment

Colin and Mog Ball

Writers and Readers Publishing Cooperative
in association with **Chameleon**

Bill Taylor, formerly development officer of the British Association of Settlements, more recently organiser at the Simba Project, in London, died while this book was being prepared for publication, in April 1979. Since Bill Taylor knew about working with young people, and since we learned a great deal about it from him, this book is dedicated to his memory.

First Edition
Published by Writers and Readers Publishing Cooperative,
9-19 Rupert Street, London W1V 7FS
in association with Chameleon,
22 Bicester Road, Richmond, Surrey

Typeset by The New Opportunity Press Limited, London.
Printed and bound in Great Britain
by Staples Printers Limited, London, Rochester.

case ISBN 0 906495 13 X
paper ISBN 0 906495 12 1

KING ALFRED'S COLLEGE
WINCHESTER

—

To be returned on or before the day marked
below:—

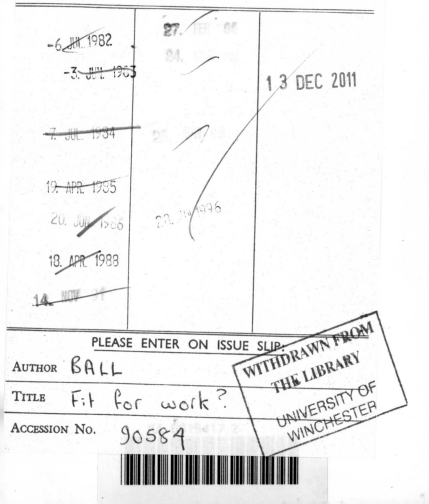

-6. JUL. 1982

-3. JUL. 1983

27. FEB. 86

24.

1 3 DEC 2011

7. JUL. 1984

19. APR. 1985

20. JUN 1986

22. JUL 1996

18. APR. 1988

14. NOV

Fit for Work?
Youth, school and (un)employment

Colin and Mog Ball

Preface

We took a number of steps on the way to writing this book, some in a deliberate effort to collect material for it. In particular, that meant interviewing approximately sixty young people who were soon to leave school, or who had recently left it, in the North-East, the East and West Midlands. The majority of those we spoke to were from the category variously described as: the unqualified, young school leavers, the disadvantaged, even 'the bottom of the barrel'. Without a doubt our sample was both small *and* unrepresentative of all the young people in the, say, 14-18 range.

The other steps we have taken, which were not part of the active design of this book, but rather things we happened to be doing before and during the time of writing it, have helped us to place these young people and what they told us on a firmer footing. Three years ago we produced a study of young people as volunteers, and in the course of producing that we interviewed a larger number of young people. We have made use of that material in this book, because much of what they said was about themselves as well as what they were doing. In addition we have made use of published material, particularly surveys and studies of young people, in and out of school and work, which are far more 'statistically valid' than anything we have been able to carry out ourselves. What we have done is simply to *talk* to young people and record every word they say.

We have also been able to talk to many people who work with and for young people. Again, some of this contact was purposely undertaken in order to provide material for this book. The greater amount was the result of the fact that for the past four years we have worked for two government departments. Through this work we have met large numbers of people in the youth, community and employment-related fields. When, as a result of the hours you spend talking to people in those fields, learning what they are doing and what they are feeling, you write a book, that leaves you with a heavy sense of responsibility. Some of these people will be outraged. Perhaps they entirely disagree, you have got them all wrong, you have pinched their ideas, perhaps even screwed up those ideas in translation. Whatever they may think about the end-product, we would like to acknowledge the help these people have given us, and to assure those who may feel that there is criticism of them implicit in some of our comments, that this is not personal criticism.

Finally, we have been influenced by others who have written about school, about work, and about the links and transitions between the two; about the nature of institutions and public services, about youth and unemployment and about the nature of work. Occasionally we quote from their writings, but we have tried, with frequent reminders from our editor, Jonathan Croall, to stick to three tasks: to let young people speak through this book; to put their views and experience in a wider setting; to say what we consider is wrong with the present state of affairs and what can and should be done about it.

In other work that we have based on interviews, we have simply quoted from the people we talked to and interpreted and analysed their words, setting them in a wider context. This time we have added our own views and ideas, mainly because we are deeply concerned about the inadequacies of the ways young people are treated today, here and in other industrialised societies. We hope our personal opinions do not detract or distract from what others are saying in this book. And we hope that those we have talked to will not feel that we have distorted or misused their words merely to fit conveniently any of our own thoughts.

It remains simply to thank the many people who have helped us to write this book.

Introduction

Some years ago we wrote our first book. It was about the ways in which young people, schools and communities could develop relationships and learn from one another. There seemed to be a good deal of potential in this development, and it was being expressed practically in the growth of community service and community education. Community service meant that young people could get involved in community and institutional life outside their schools, and community education meant, ideally, the reverse process: people outside schools could get involved in the life of educational institutions.

We were concerned that the education of young people shouldn't just take place *in* the community, as they did their community service, but that the young people doing it should be more than the passive recipients of other people's knowledge and experience. They must have a positive and valued role to play. It seemed to us that young people were often the victims of adult protection and condescension — and they were victims even when the protection was very well-meaning, more so when it wasn't. We haven't changed our minds about that.

So we suggested that young people had something to contribute, and that it be contributed in a way that was relevant to their learning, and which made their learning relevant. It is one thing to be taught about issues like disability, in the same way as you are taught about sulphuric acid, but if young people are to grow and mature, they need experiences which are *real,* and that's quite another thing. Real experience is not taught in class-rooms. It is de-valued if it becomes a game. It cannot be discovered by looking over somebody else's shoulder.

Alongside that, we felt that community education should mean more than simply allowing the community into educational institutions for yoga and yoghurt-making classes. The community needed a real *role* in the institutionalised aspects of education, as well as 'out-of-school' activities like community service and the school summer fete. People had something to offer schools, and needed a proper job to do in them. We feel that as strongly now as we did then.

So we were arguing for new roles for young people in the community; new roles for the community — parents, plumbers, doctors, senior citizens, young adults, everybody — in the education process.

To make that more than fine-sounding theory and to persuade people to do something about it, we had to say more. Firstly, there were the practical details which would help the development of these fresh roles. That meant talking about structures, attitudes and resources. At the same time there were the obstacles to this development. Those things like professional elusiveness: 'This is my business, so keep out — and anyway you're neither qualified nor trained . . .'; and institutional inflexibility: 'These ideas are all very well, but we have to be responsible for . . .'

Since we were talking about opening up the education business, we wanted to write a book that everybody could read. We thought we had something to say to people other than teachers and social workers. We hoped young people themselves might read it. Was it inevitable that we ended up with a much more exclusive market? Student teachers enjoyed it, on the whole. Some young teachers enjoyed it. A few older teachers found it interesting.

Maybe that was inevitable. But this time we are determined to try even harder to reach a wider audience. This time the problem is a public, not a professional or political one. Professional and political response to this problem will not be adequate. It is too big to hand over.

In this book we examine how young people are prepared for the lives they will lead when they leave schools. How do young people in school see that life? What is done to make this so-called 'transition' come about? Who are the people managing it? Who should be managing it? What are the roles of these people? What are the roles of young people? What should these roles be?

We use the word 'role' to mean a 'useful function'. And we have said 'so-called transition' because it seems to us to be a misleading word, suggesting a limited period of time. Talk about 'transition' and many people, especially professional people, will assume that you are talking about 'transition from school to work'. Now so far we have not managed to mention work. It will also be assumed that 'transition' refers to a period immediately before and immediately after leaving school to go to work, as opposed to going to college. We are not limiting our subject to this period. Instead we will look at a longer time span than 14-19 years, or 16-19 years.

Our main objection to 'transition' is that it implies the existence of two worlds, school and after-school, which are totally different and bound to be so. After-school, after life — is leaving school a kind of dying? School is sheltered, secure, protected. After-school is altogether harsher, a ruthless and exposed place. You're on your own there. That's the way it may be, and that's why expressions like 'transition' are familiar. But part of our argument will be that such brutish change is not useful, and doesn't have to happen.

So we are not just talking about 'preparation for the world of work' or 'transition' into it. We are talking about 'growing up'. That means a good deal more than being prepared for work, and indicates a steady movement from childhood and total dependence — a period officially assumed to last at least until the age of sixteen — to a position where the individual is confident, mature and independent. This condition is not reached automatically when you leave school.

But whatever adults may think, this is a question which is very important to young people. Who am I? What am I for? What can I do? Why do parents have children? If the answer to that last one is that we have them to care for, protect and love, what do we tell them when that stops? Somewhere along the line the dependent child needs to learn that he or she has something to contribute, that there is a role for them.

Part of this book will be about the factors which help or hinder the discovery of role. They vary from structures, attitudes and resources to professional and institutional barriers. And the factors which inhibit young people in discovering who they are and what they can do are the same as those limiting people of all ages.

Clearly all this is closely allied to what we talked about in our first book. The participation of young people with other people in the community and outside school, is a significant contribution to their growing up, if this participation comes about for the right reasons. Since it is one of the ways young people in schools can have a real function, we shall talk about the community service field in this book, too.

But there are other matters, ideas and examples of practice which must be assembled if we are going to make our point. Many of these have been treated separately in the past. They include work experience schemes, youth work, apprentice-learning, careers teaching, school/industry links, community education. There is also the Great Debate, the Raising of the School Leaving Age, the Manpower Services Commission, the Careers Service and the equally important political education, unemployment, training, trade unions, social education, life and social skills, job-searching. Some of these matters don't seem to be connected. We hope to show that they are. We also hope to explain what they are or do, and how they co-exist, comfortably or otherwise.

Many questions will be raised as we go along, and some of them will be explored as they arise. Others may be put on one side, to be examined later in the book, in the part where answers and ideas may come more readily than they would earlier on.

1 Youth as a Problem

There is one set of questions that immediately comes up when the schooling of young people is the subject of discussion. What is the function of a school? Should it prepare young people for examinations? For work? (Or unemployment?) For life? For after-school? What relative importance do schools attach to each of these? What importance should they have? What do young people feel prepares them? Does preparing mean the same as 'growing up'? Or is it a form of processing? Or is it to do with releasing potential? What do young people feel helps them to grow up? What do employers expect of those leaving school? What do those leaving school expect?

Anybody who is working with young people at some stage in that child-to-adult period will feel that the answers to questions like 'What is the function of a school?' are obvious. After all, there are vast structures, employing thousands of people, which are founded on answers to them, and which could not function without some kind of bedrock of belief. Practice is founded on the answers to these questions.

But certain evidence suggests that current practice does not work. When this is made public, and that happens regularly every couple of months or so, usually on the back of some piece of research, or some local scandal, influencing factors are blamed. Schools blame parents, policemen blame social workers, industrialists blame schools, parents blame 'that crowd you've got mixed up with'.

The education debate

This shifting around of blame allows current solutions to gain credibility. The 'Great Debate' began about the content of education, at a time when politicians felt it was a good idea to show concern for this area. Self-interests jostled and manoeuvred, but neither young people themselves, nor interested outsiders, got a word in edgeways. Either they couldn't express what they wanted to say, or they couldn't make themselves heard. As the issues began to sound very complicated, it was hard to know where to begin.

From this Debate a 'back-to-basics' movement began to emerge. Poor literacy and numeracy among young people at or leaving school were ascribed to curricula that were too wide-ranging. Too much energy was being wasted on fringe concerns — 'liberal education', and that sort of thing.

Even as the political centre raised this debate about standards, the political right found another raw nerve — discipline. They agreed that standards, as measured by the ability to read, write and count, were falling. But they also felt that behavioural standards, evidenced by football violence, vandalism and mugging, were falling too. So they called for 'back-to-basics' in discipline. Stricter regimes were needed in school, and in the family and the community. The urge to conservatism in the content of education was paralleled by the urge to conservatism in method.

It's easy to dismiss these ideas. But there are clues in them to the real reasons why current practice in education is failing. The debate about the content of education indicates one positive thing. We must find out what is useful and relevant to young people. But what is relevant in school-learning terms is not the same thing as what is relevant to growing up. And an overdose of basics is liable to be as fatal as an over-dose of wide-ranging 'liberal education'. If the shrill pronouncements about discipline say anything positive, it is that everybody, including young people, needs a clearer perception of the place and identity young people have in the community.

It's horrible not to know who you are. It's confusing and demoralising to be functionless. Yet that is the state that young people enjoy. Institutions established to care and nurture them maintain this state and applaud themselves for doing so. But is there some magic day in adolescence when young people change from being dependent children to being independent adults? Such magic days may be enshrined in law, but that is only for administrative convenience. Individual experience suggests that maturing hasn't got anything to do with the statute book. But the advocates of stronger discipline are not offering young people a role, just another vacuum. Young people are in a vacuum as it is, but at least many of the people who administer it care deeply about them, and baulk at the idea of harsher regimes.

The inadequacy of school as a preparation for work

There is a need to burrow deeper to get at the really basic

questions. Content and discipline, what is taught and the way in which we deal with young people, are not the only issues which point to this. Another one has to do with the preparation and processing of young people for work. It is here that current practice is most clearly seen to fail and it is here that educationists must wonder if they have found the right answers to that set of questions.

There is a high level of unemployment. It is particularly high among young people, and it is highest of all among those young people who do not succeed at school, and who leave it ill-equipped to succeed either in employment or unemployment. They are ill-equipped in two ways. First of all, they are having to emerge from the cocoon of dependence, the functionless vacuum, into a harsh and competitive world where they have to stand on their own feet, be self-reliant.

There is a lot to be said for learning and growing coming out of just that experience: dealing with the unknown. But to expect that kind of learning to begin at sixteen years is expecting a lot. As a first taste of learning by experience it comes rather late. And what an experience to learn from! To say 'You're on your own, survive!' to an individual who has had to bring notes to say why she couldn't do P.E., or who hasn't been allowed to vault over a horse in the gym without supervision, that's a dramatic about-turn. We have talked to many young people about to leave school, or in their first year out of school, and we hope to show just how traumatic this change really is to them.

As well as this lack of self-reliance among young people who leave school, there is also a lack, among many, of the most basic skills to offer an employer. We don't know exactly how many young people are ill-equipped in this way, too, but they're often called 'the bottom 30%'. So even though they have not had much opportunity to learn by experience, because the emphasis in the education up to now has been on cognitive learning — the facts and skills — even that hasn't worked for these 30%ers. The content debaters say that this is because there hasn't been enough attention to those basic skills; the others say 'They haven't learned because they haven't been made to learn'. Industry blames schools for turning out such poor material for the work force. More blame is shifted around.

On the political front a comparison between free capitalist economies and state-controlled socialist economies reveals an embarrassment. Youth unemployment is higher in the former systems, in the developed world, at least. British trade unions must also find it embarrassing that the employment protection legislation for which they have striven has a nasty side effect. Employers are more reluctant than they used to be to take on unknown quantities, like young people. It's harder to get rid of them now, if you make a mistake. Do we blame employers, because they're not prepared to take a chance? Or do we blame the government, the legislators? Or the unions, the lobby? And what of the suggestion made by the British Youth Council and other bodies, that if overtime working was eliminated completely there would be enough jobs for everyone? It seems that people with jobs are quick to put their own interests ahead of those of their younger brothers, especially when their own jobs are safe. Who would strike against a company which was making no effort to take on young workers?

Technological development is reducing the number of jobs in many industrial sectors, and, at the same time, dividing the work force into an elite — who work at the core of these new technologies, with the skills they require — and the rest, on the fringe, in jobs which require fewer, if any skills. In a supermarket in the United States you can see this latter development in practice. To work at the check-out counter you don't need to read or count. Lines are printed on every item bought, and these are fed through electric circuitry which prints out the bill. This eliminates error, but it also eliminates the need for any human contribution at all. Payment? There are devices which present the correct change automatically. They are familiar already, and coming shortly is the till which can spot a bad cheque or an over-used credit card. So the need for that little bit of social intercourse will soon disappear as well.

That makes the call for 'back-to-basics' look rather over-simplified. If we were to treat the subject of this book, the growth and development of young people from children into adults, solely in the context of schools and the recognised 'education system' we might as well not bother. What is the point of learning and developing towards the 'world of work', to be inherited at 16, when the 'world of work' doesn't need the skills you've been busy acquiring? How much attention has been given to your survival in the 'world without work?' And what about the 'world *outside* work' which nobody may have mentioned to you much at all, even though it increases in importance as the availability of what we call work changes rapidly.

Many of our institutions and much of the way we live seem to hinder rather than encourage young people's growing up. Is it possible that many grow up *in spite* of what we do to them? If this is the case, what can we do about it? What new styles and processes are necessary?

The dominance of institutions

To answer these questions we must make a leap in our imagination. We are not used to looking at a social problem and saying 'There is a need. What actions, institutional, collective, individual, must we take to meet this need?' Instead, we make an automatic step, from recognising 'the need for provision' to meeting it solely with 'institutional action'.

The reasons for this automatic step are partly political. Institutional action is visible, and there's political capital to be gleaned from it. Then there is the self-interest of the professionals who deliver the services of the institution. As new needs are discovered, they will try to be responsible for the 'discovery' and to extend their own operation to deal with the problem.

Professionals are specialists in large units of production. We know that they are remote, often intimidating, that they set their own standards and, because they claim 'expertise', are difficult to judge or control. But professionals in institutions are accepted as the most cost-effective way to organise the population when it is not earning its living. And we shouldn't forget that institutional action is easy to organise. But the nastiest reason for relying on it to deal with all social needs is that, since wage-slavery and human nature are considered to have reduced us all to self-interested creatures, institutions are a way of caring without having to do anything about needs and problems ourselves. The society which responds to needs with institutional action alone divides itself into 'providers', who are the institution, 'clients', who have the needs and problems, and the rest of us. We are the onlookers. Institutional action is expansionist — it wants as many clients as possible, and it is powerful and exclusive. It knows what is good for us.

The limits to institutional response and growth in the post-war years have come because of lack of money. A fundamental principle of public service institutions is that *more* equals *better*. *More* means more of the policy to which they subscribe, which they have been practising for a long time, and which they see as the right way. So more school, more teachers, mean better education. This policy finds alternatives to its practice very difficult to live with. If these alternatives work, meeting needs in a non-institutional way, by collective or individual action, and really *meeting* needs, it is common for the public service to take them over and incorporate them in 'the policy'.

Professionals who work with the growing young recognise several 'needs' which they see themselves as meeting. These needs are dealt with separately, depending on the responsibility of the professional. If it's an out-of-school, social need, then that's the youth worker's sphere. If it's finding a job, then there's the careers officer. When professionals want to attract resources to their sphere, they are inclined to re-name the needs of young people and call them 'problems'. When they say 'We want to do more about this problem' they usually mean that they want to appoint more staff.

It is important to talk about the exclusive nature of need-meeting and problem-solving. Perhaps we will be able to convey just how fragmented it all is when seen from the outside — by a young person, say?

'I feel very worried about the future. Nobody seems to *know* anything about what you can do. They just give you advice and they say "I can only advise you, it's up to you to get a job in the end". I wish they'd leave me alone now and let me get on with it. I do feel very confused.'

2 Coping with Youth: In School

A youth is strong enough, able enough and knows enough to do things which earn either money, respect or both. He or she may not be able to do them as well or as quickly as an adult, but they can do them. Youth begins when we stop the child from doing useful and harmless things. That is, when we make decisions on behalf of a person who is capable of deciding things for themselves. Youth should be about making decisions, but usually it isn't.

We prefer to pretend that youth has not arrived. It seems easier for childhood to continue; and the growing child often finds this easier too, for a while, and acquiesces. But as capabilities become more obvious, friction develops with those who treat the youth as child. This sixteen-year-old boy is in his last term at a comprehensive school. He has a Saturday job, which he mentions in this description of an argument with his father:

'I often have rows with him, but before he just used to hit me with a slipper. A couple of weeks ago I'd just come from work about eleven o'clock at night and he says "Your hair's mucky". I says, "It ain't, it's just a bit dusty". He said I'd to get it washed, and when I'd done it I went to the mirror to comb it, and went like that. (Gestures.) He just come up and smacked me straight in the ear, and then he beats me in the mouth. Me mum's funny, because as soon as he comes home she'll say "Oh John, he's been cheeky," and all that, but as soon as he starts hitting me she says "Oh don't, you'll hurt him."'

His father says, 'While he's living in this house he'll do what I say.' Later quotations from this sixteen-year-old will show that other adults, notably teachers, are treating him in a similar way to his father.

The relationship between this young man and his father shows a common ambivalence in the attitude of adults to youth:

'When me Dad goes on at me I say "I haven't been in trouble with the police". I think he's proud of me for that, really, though he doesn't say so. Me mate's just left school and he did a job and got caught — it's not worth it.'

We are pleased when youths express self-confidence and self-reliance in socially acceptable ways, we call them "delinquents" if it comes out in anti-social behaviour and actions. But we expect youths to act like youths, as opposed to children, and we treat them like children. If they do not act like youths, we presume that it is because we are not treating them like children *enough*. So we elaborate our care systems, and make more and more decisions for youth, and try to suffocate it, or, at least, to delay its onset.

But adults who try to perpetuate childhood are not the only influence on growing youth. There will also be development and growth through contact with peers, others who do not treat the youth as a child, and the environment. The young school leaver who has already spoken, shows how these influences can work. His Saturday job is at a car-breakers' yard:

'Last summer I wanted a job, so I thought "I'll go up there and try". The bloke who owns it comes down and says, "Can I help you?" and I says, "Got any spare time job?" and he says "Come back next Saturday". The first time I went there and he says: "What are you going to do about that car there?" He was standing there with his girlfriend, it was dead embarrassing. But I chopped the car down in about half an hour and he says, "You've done this before, haven't you?" I really like him. I hadn't done it before, but I thought, when I'd taken all the spares, that the best thing to do was to chop the roof off, so I just chopped it through the middle. He says, "That's good, that is". I was right glad.'

That employer was a young man of twenty-five himself. He hasn't been trained to teach or care, and his attitude does not seek to perpetuate the child-status of his employee, but rather helps him to grow up. But why do the systems which aim to teach and care seem to end up perpetuating childhood and stifling youth?

The youth business

The answer is simple. The perpetuation of childhood and the postponement of adulthood are multi-million pound businesses. Most people, called on to define youth, would do so in terms of this business. Youth are in youth clubs and secondary schools, being cared for and serviced by people trained to that function. Other aspects of human existence have become enshrined in the business which services them. Ivan Illich has put this in a historical context:

> 'At first, new knowledge is applied to the solution of a clearly stated problem, and scientific measuring sticks are applied to account for the new efficiency. But at a second point the progress demonstrated in a previous achievement is used as a rationale for the exploitation of society as a whole in the service of a value which is determined and constantly revised by an element of society, by one of its self-certifying professional elites . . .' *(Tools for Conviviality)*

It is not just the professional elite of the youth business which determines the treatment that young people should receive. Most adults are party to youth suffocation in some form or other. In societies with divided labour functions, parents do not have all the knowledge which needs to be taught. So the children are brought together to learn from teachers. The parent is free to work at functions where the presence of children would be a hindrance. Then there is a second stage. It is the teacher, or the self-certifying professional elite to which the teacher belongs, which determines what, how and for how long this learning and child-minding should go on. It is not 'society' which determines this. But 'society' does not object to these decisions because we all find it convenient for childhood to continue. Who hasn't breathed a sigh of relief at the end of the summer holidays? Yet here is a description of modern childhood which puts those sighs into context:

> 'By the institution of childhood I mean all those attitudes and feelings and also customs and laws, that put a great gulf or barrier between the young and their elders, and the world of their elders; that make it difficult or impossible for young people to make contact with the larger society around them and, even more, to play any kind of active, responsible, useful part in it; that lock the young into eighteen years or more of subserviency and dependency and make them . . . a mixture of expensive nuisance, fragile treasure, slave and super-pet . . .' (John Holt, *Escape from Childhood)*

Youth is when children begin not to need us, and then they begin to do 'our' work. Parents often look forward to the day when 'he can stand on his own two feet'. But when they are faced with a young person doing just that, what happens? The sixteen-year-old we quoted before has arranged a job to go to when he leaves school. It is at the yard where he does his Saturday job. He is extremely

pleased about this, and given the shortage of jobs in his area, he has
done well to find one:

> 'I never come to school yesterday afternoon and the teacher
> phoned up home. Me Dad had just come home from work in a
> bad mood and he started on at me and said I should pack me
> bags and leave home and got all upset. And then he says, "You
> can't go up the yard, never again". He says he wouldn't care if I
> went on the dole, but he can't stop me taking this job, can he? He
> says I can wait until I'm eighteen. But he can't stop me, can he? I
> wanted to talk to somebody about it, because it's a job, and it's
> better to have a job than nothing, isn't it? Me mate said last night
> that me Dad's jealous, he thinks he's getting old. He's only forty-
> two.'

The father in this saga is suggesting that his son continue at school.
He is not excited or pleased by the confidence and self-reliance his
son has shown by finding a job. He is not the only one who doesn't
want this young man to become an employed adult. Teachers at
school have advised him against taking the job, but this advice does
not stem from the recognition of real achievement in school. As a
school pupil the speaker was poor:

> 'I've never been very good at writing, you know. I can write, but
> I've always liked the practical side best — mechanics and
> metalwork. But the teachers make you write, and they say you
> should work harder and they talk about all the exams I could
> have done. None of me mates are doing exams either. The
> teacher said I don't look further than the end of my nose. He said
> he couldn't see the firm I'm going to work for making it.'

Nobody seems to be encouraging this young man at all. But then
there is his employer, the one person who doesn't seem threatened
by his incipient adulthood, the one person who needs him to grow
up.

The teachers here are part of a huge job creation programme
which suffocates youth. It is followed closely by those programmes
which care for children who have tried to throw off the constricting
clothes we like to dress them in.

Rejecting the youth business

Divesting yourself of the insignia of dependence is frightening, of
course. Young people know they may find themselves very exposed

without the paraphernalia which signal their childhood to the world. But many between the ages of six and sixteen do show signs of dissatisfaction with their status as the provided for and cared for. An increasing number are frustrated, and they do different things to make it clear. They may *reject* school, or family, or other institutions which have been set up to look after them, like the police.

A survey carried out for the Headmasters' Association and the Headmasters' Conference in 1974 found that at one in seven comprehensives and one in six secondary moderns, more than 2% of the pupils truanted for half of the week, every week. In 10% of these schools, more than 10% of the pupils only bothered to attend school four days out of five every week. The survey noted that truancy rates were higher in large schools and that such schools had higher proportions of 'disruptive' pupils.

The 1976 report of the National Child Development Study (which followed the lives of some 17,000 children born in the week March 3-9 1958) detailed what was happening to the group in their sixteenth year (1974). We shall refer to this excellent study elsewhere in this book. On truancy, it said:

'. . . teachers were asked whether the description "truants from school" applied to the study child, on the basis of behaviour in the past twelve months. This was said . . . to "apply somewhat" to 12%, and "certainly apply" to 8%. Thus one fifth of these children were felt by their teachers to have truanted to some extent in the past year and for one in twelve truancy was presumably thought to be fairly frequent.' (Ken Fogelman (ed.), *Britain's Sixteen Year Olds)*

This study also sought the views of parents and of young people themselves. Of the parents:

'88% said that their child had not played truant in the last year, 10% said that they had done so occasionally and 3% said that they had truanted at least once per week.'

This seems to give a lower figure than that of the teachers, and for some reason it adds up to 101%. But the major discrepancy lies not between the parental and teacher perception of the problem, but between both of them and the young people themselves. When they were asked the question 'Have you stayed away from school at all this year, when you should have been there?' an astounding 52% answered 'Yes'.

In our own conversations with young people, the question of truanting came up time and again. Everybody seemed to have done it once, at least. Here is a typical description of what it's like, from a fifteen year old girl who often spends weeks at a time like this:

'Once you're in the town, or in the swimming baths across the road, you can spend the afternoon there instead of school. Or in the public toilets: you go down the toilets and see loads of 'em.'

Another girl had somewhere to go:

'I used to have a mate up in the flats, and her mum used to go out to work and we used to go up there and wag in there. The flats are opposite the school, so we used to keep our eye on the school. It was boring in a way, but we used to find things to do, like get a pack of cards out or do her mum's washing.'

The response to this rejection of school is to treat young people as sinners, as though they are to blame. In order to persuade them to be better people and to stop rejecting all this loving care, society offers *more care*.

For school rejectors — or school phobics as they are called — there are special centres. Some of these do recognise that perhaps the deluded child is looking for some alternative to the school which he or she has rejected. But most aim to get the children back to where they came from. The idea is to help them adjust. 'Case conferences' of teachers, social workers and child psychologists meet to refine the caring process.

For the home rejectors there are also counsellors and social workers and care and supervision orders. If the government hadn't been so tight-fisted there would have been more advice booths at main line stations and more posters saying 'Don't go to London'. But many home rejectors don't get that far. They just stay out without telling us where they are, they mutter under their breath when we remind them to tidy their rooms, they don't want to come with us on the family holiday. Our solution to rejection is to insist on physical presence. Stay and be cared for.

Another sign of dissatisfaction is more violent and anti-social: vandalism and other kinds of juvenile crime, or just plain assertive behaviour, whether it takes the form of punk rock or aggressive horseplay in the street. All of this costs a good deal of money every year, not just in putting right damage, but elaborating the care systems we hope will stop it happening. But exasperation does set in and the elaboration of care is often criticised for not working.

There is 'intermediate treatment' to divert the young crypto-offender, community service court orders to make the punishment fit the crime, and if all else fails, there is good old-fashioned detention.

Although the system is devised to keep youth in a place where it can be protected, cared for, provided for and generally suffocated, it is nevertheless a divided system. This fragmentation is useful, because it means that when the whole business is failing, one bit of it can blame another. In an old report on truancy and vandalism produced by the National Association of Schoolmasters we remember that it was all the fault of 'pop culture, the media, and the "do-good" approach of social workers.'

A third piece of evidence for the frustration of youth is often forgotten. But it is widespread, can be seen on the street every day, especially after four o'clock, at weekends and during the holidays. Everywhere there are inarticulate, incoherent, immature young people, who know little about how to deal with themselves, with us and with the world around them. We say we don't want young people to be like this. We want them to be articulate, able, mature and self-reliant, but helping them get that way is too difficult, and aren't we a bit frightened of the consequences? Aren't growing young people a threat? Whatever the reason we respond with care and more care. If only we had a better pupil/teacher ratio! If only we had more careers officers! If only we had more youth clubs! If only we could get rid of archaic school buildings and have bright fresh surroundings for the children to play in! If only we could make the summer playscheme longer this year! If only we could have done more about intermediate treatment before money got so short! Language labs, swimming pools, skateboard rinks, adventure playgrounds . . . .

In the rest of this chapter we want to look at the provision-for-youth business, try to show the pressures of extended childhood, and put the institutions into context, in the overall field of provision in society.

The school experience

Going to school removes children from the mainstream of social activity. Between the ages of six and sixteen young people will spend about seven hours a day in a school. That is more than half their waking hours. That will happen for five days a week and about 36 weeks a year. Almost all of that time will be spent with a small group of other children of similar age. In some cases they will be of similar sex also. In the early years, until they reach nine, ten or eleven, children in school have *activities,* they 'do' things. But right from the beginning, and for most of the time after they reach the age of eleven, they will be *learning* or *studying.*

In the school context, it is the learning or studying which are called 'work'. This is interesting as verbal usage. What is called 'work' in school is different from what is called 'work' in the outside world. We have discovered some confusion among children in secondary schools when we have asked them what they understand by 'work'. What they describe, in answer to this question, is always *school* work. Here's an example of such an exchange, with a fourteen year old girl in her third year at a comprehensive school.

What is work?
'Do you mean subjects and that? Or do you mean what do you do it for and that? I think it's working yourself up to a good job. If you work hard at school you'll get a good career.'

Most young people we talked to did not see certain school subjects as 'work'. P.E. and domestic science were often quoted here. In these subjects teachers are less inclined to say 'Get on with your work'. In them children are not so likely to be at desks and writing, so they don't day-dream and need to be reminded to concentrate quite so much. But most study is done from books, under the direction of the teacher.

Even on its own terms, this is a pretty inefficient business. The seven hours per day in school includes something like 1½ hours of break-time, and of the remaining 5½ hours, almost an hour may be lost in beginning and ending lessons. So, allowing for a fair wind, about 4½ hours may be spent on learning. The foul winds may emanate from the 'small group of children of similar age', since those who find the work difficult or boring may disrupt the lesson a little, because they can't understand it or simply don't wish to. These children may be segregated into 'streams'.

Now for the subject matter of those lessons. English and Mathematics — stories and number work in the early years: there's no escaping them. Then there will be science and history, geography and games, languages and art. It would be nice to think that all these subjects will be useful, and that is why they are taught. That's partly true. It is useful to be able to read and write and count, to know about nature, about our long culture, and about our country and others. It's really useful to know another language, though preferably one you'll get a chance to use sometimes. Of course it's useful to cook and sew, make things and mend them; it's healthy and satisfying to play games.

But usefulness is a spin-off from school subjects, rather than their primary aim. Learning subjects, however useful, is necessary in school because children can be examined on them. If they pass these examinations they will receive certificates which will enable them to go on and learn more. The certificates also have a useful spin-off, because they say something about the child who is leaving the school and looking for a job. But what they say is of limited importance and relates to success in learning school subjects.

So central are examinations to our system of schooling, and so important are they to teachers, that they become an essential, to be sat at all costs. This may have something to do with the fact that teachers have to pass exams to become teachers. But in recent years young people have been told that unless they sit and pass examinations their chances of getting paid work when they leave school will be lessened. Remember how the third form girl told us that if you work hard at school you'll get a good career? She went on to say:

> 'But even if you work hard and get good CSEs and O levels and that, it doesn't always mean you'll get a job.'

And her friend, a girl of the same age, said:

> 'There's so many people telling you to get qualifications so as you'll get the jobs easier, so you get the qualifications and then you can't get jobs, just stupid jobs you hate. They are encouraging too many people to get qualifications and in the end there's not enough jobs left for them.'

More grist to that particular mill comes from the sixteen year old boy, whose experience at home we've already heard about:

> 'It's a waste of time when you've been taught history for three years, and then you don't do owt with it. They're always saying about how you need your qualifications and everything, but me mate's brother only left school with a couple of CSE's and he's had about six jobs — as soon as he got his licence he swopped jobs. It's not qualifications you need, it's a driving licence.'

Many young people are pressed by their school teachers to take examinations, even when they do not wish to do them. The following comment is from a sixteen year old girl who has decided to leave school at the first opportunity:

'The careers teacher wants me to make a career for myself where I don't really mind what kind of job I get as long as I like it. She says she doesn't want me just to go in for any old job because she says I've got the brains to do something better.'

This girl is in a similar position:

'All the teachers say they are disappointed, really, in me. They say I should think of something better than just going out and getting a job. They say they're disappointed, that I should stop on and do exams, and they, like, reject you, sort of thing.'

The language which the teachers used is interesting. They could do better, teachers are disappointed.

The school system of learning and studying, of examination and 'qualification', rests on an assumption that these are both good and useful to *all young people*. These processes are the principal object of schools as institutions, within the overall task of childminding and dependence stimulation. It would not be fair to say that they are the sole object, however. There are other things that schools try to do. Of this principal object it is enough to point out that schools teach in order that children will learn, and that they will learn things which will help them, primarily, to go on and learn more things, and which will help them, secondarily, to get a job. (But which will have, incidentally, little use within whatever job they do unless they, perchance, become teachers, too.) The things they learn may have some vague utility for them, as a child, or as an adult, as part of their 'interests'.

. Some young people like learning and studying very much. This may be because of their age, interest or aptitude. They may not like the part where they are examined on what they learn, but they like the actual business of learning. For some it is an across-the-board joy, for others it is more specific, and limited to music, or maths or whatever. Other young people don't like it, but manage it, adjusting to the fact that there's no alternative. The management and adjustment may be self-induced, or may be encouraged by parents.

The 'new' curriculum

But what about the rest of school? Principal though the study/ examination objective is, there are other things on the learning schedule, or curriculum, as it is called, and these cannot really be called part of the learning-list. True, children will learn from them. But the nature of these subjects sometimes means that it is impossible to 'examine' them. And some others are purposely not examined because they are not considered acceptable to the higher learning bodies or to employers. But it is in these activities, which are different from academic 'subjects', that another, unmentioned side of learning can be seen. Learning of this kind is often called 'affective' learning, in teachers' language. That contrasts it with 'cognitive' learning, of facts and skills. 'Affective' learning is about feelings and emotions.

These subjects have names like social education, social studies, community studies, modern studies, environmental studies, humanities and environmental education. These titles have a weighty sound, and study is proclaimed as an essential part of them so that no one should think they are a skive. In some schools there are urban studies or black studies on the curricula, and community service, too, comes into this category. And often nowadays you will find child care and child development on the timetable. Most of these subjects and courses, these new 'studies' are a phenomenon of the past two decades. They appear to have been introduced for two main reasons.

First, schools, and bodies concerned with the development of the curriculum, recognised that the cognitive curriculum was in many ways unrelated to the lives of young people and, at a more general level, that schools were divorced from the hum and throb of what was actually going on around them. There was some understanding of that comment about it being a waste of time learning history and then not doing owt with it. Many kids were saying it, after all, and teachers and administrators would have had to plead deafness not to have responded to that chorus of 'What's the *use* of . . . (history, science, geometry, anything)?' So the hum and throb of the world around the school, whether that meant a war in the Middle East, or a new motorway planned for the local area, was introduced into the classroom. The word used is relevance, for this sort of development. School 'subjects' are made relevant to the lives of children in schools.

Secondly, these new developments were boosted by the 'problem of the early leavers', alternatively known as the 'less able' or 'non-academics'. Some children do not adjust well to the academic, fact-oriented curriculum, and either resent it or reject it. So these new subjects were thought particularly suitable for them, the 'non-academics'.

Some of the old 'academic' subjects lost their clearly defined edges. Because, as their names imply, these subjects took as their starting points the *community*, the *environment, social* issues, and, indeed, the individual herself or himself. Environmental studies, for example, is largely concerned with our physical environment, so into that new pot goes some of your old geography and biology. We will not attempt to describe all of these subjects, and what they have absorbed from the more traditional curriculum, because interpretation and usage varies from school to school and from teacher to teacher. But it is noticeable that schools in the private sector haven't taken to them in an enthusiastic way, particularly when they are schools which cherish their 'academic success rate'.

These subjects had potential. At least they gave the individual student a chance to be a part of the subject. Everybody is, after all, part of the community and environment. So the new subjects were distinguished from the old academic list and especially from those subjects which were about facts rather than skills. In these subjects the individual was an onlooker — there was no personal involvement with sulphuric acid, unless you spilt it on your shirt. But the message that personal involvement was needed had got through to the professionals who introduced the new subjects. It seemed like a way to conquer disaffection with school: 'Look, school's about you and your life — it matters.'

But as these subjects are treated in schools, much of their potential has not been realised. Many teachers have simply turned the new subjects into neo-academic, fact-finding and rote-learning exercises. And these exercises, under their new titles, aren't even recognised by others outside school as qualifications. The comment about history being a waste of time was made by a lad who doesn't have history on his school time-table, but who is not duped by fancy names. He knows what he is getting is history, whatever it's called, and he thinks it is a waste of time.

So the word 'relevance' is rather dubious when it is exemplified by these studies. And we should not forget for whom they were deemed suitable — the 'less able'. This girl knows the difference between 'relevance' and usefulness:

'Another useless thing we learnt in social studies this year was pre-school learning: what kind of toys kids play with and all that — it was daft.'

However, some of the innovations were not easily emasculated. They, too, were only considered suitable for this specific, non-academic group, but sometimes they caught the interest of young people and were considered useful by them. Social education is one of these. It has to involve the individual in the subject, because the individual *is* most of the subject.

In essence it means learning about yourself, about other people, closely or less closely related to yourself, like your parents, family, other people in the community, and, more importantly, how you can adjust and relate to them, given the fact that they, like you, have their own idiosyncracies. The subject is also about skills, but skills quite different from the ones school have been accustomed to teaching. Skills have to be developed to understand and cope with yourself, your life, and with other people. Those are important skills. This subject has collected a new name: Life and Social Skills. It covers everything from sex and smoking to finding, presenting yourself for, getting and keeping a job, and there's more besides. But this is offered to the non-academic child. It is assumed that those continuing with education do not need to explore these issues and acquire these skills.

If social education took an 'individual outwards' approach, another of the new subjects went in the opposite direction. This was community service. The historical introduction of community service into secondary schools went like this: educationists discover philanthropy and think it might be useful, especially for keeping the non-academic children occupied. The potential of this subject is largely unrealised, but it can amount to learning by doing things. It is learning-by-doing alongside other people in the community, its institutions and organisations. Through the experience there is a chance to discover something of your own function and worth. These are important discoveries.

This girl, who habitually played truant from school, told us about her experience of community service:

'At school we used to have community service, going round helping people with their shopping, talking to people who are depressed and that. Me and my friend used to do it in our spare time. We used to know an old lady who was crippled and had something wrong with her arm — arthritis, I think it was. She couldn't go out, and we used to go round every Saturday, make her tea and dinner and take her out for half an hour. This place for old people, it's got this caretaker, and we asked if we could go in and talk to the people, because we were bored and they were depressed. So we went in and they were telling us about when they were young. That was off our own bat, doing that. But we used to go up to an old peoples' home with the school and we used to play draughts and cards. It was ever so nice, and the people were nice and all. There used to be a telly and everything, and you used to sit next to them. Some of them were a bit narky, but they were ever so glad to see us. We used to go every Friday afternoon, but we stopped doing it because somebody stole £5.'

And an unemployed young man remembered his community service work at school quite clearly:

'From school I used to go to the old people's hospital. I enjoyed that. I find that you can get on with old people more better than you can get on with the young ones. You find you can help them. We dressed them and put dressings on their wounds, get their meals, put them to bed, bath them. It was a whole day up there, sort of day-release from school, really. I started in the fifth year. All the fifth year done it. You had different courses to go on, like people picked to go to factories and that. You had a choice. I chose the hospital and found I got on rather well there.

Why did you choose the hospital?
I just fancied doing it.'

Experience as education

Many adults, when you ask how they have learned about themselves and about the world, will cite experiences.

Skills, facts, attitudes, feelings. The school, through its curriculum, has admitted an interest in all of these. It hasn't included them in the curriculum for *all* young people, and sometimes the balance and mix of them are rather odd. Even so, they are there. But experience: that's another thing.

In some schools, for some young people the learning process includes "work experience". This means spending some time, generally a small part of it, in a local factory, office, or wherever, getting the feel of a working life. This work is not paid, and generally doesn't mean actually doing much *work*. It's more looking over other people's shoulders. Community service is often called a kind of work experience but, if properly organised, the young person will *really* be doing a necessary and important job. That job may seem very menial, but it is doing *something*.

Anything which disassociates learning from the institution of school must be welcomed. It is the divorce of school from community and real life which leads to the institutionalisation of the child-youth, stranded on the purpose-built desert island that has been provided for him. Schools physically separate young people from the rest of us. Anything that puts them back is to be welcomed. Out-of-school learning of any sort is often called 'experiential learning'. But if all the learner is doing is watching over somebody's shoulder, then she's hardly gaining experience, she's not likely to be "learning by doing". And quite a lot of school work experience is merely that — watching. And again, it is offered to a limited number of young people, just as the rest of the 'new curriculum' is only meant for them. It's those non-academics again, the ones who need to be slotted into factories, shops and offices. But do we want to circumscribe the life-chances of young people in this way? Is it really enough to close the file on a school-leaver when he has a job, any job, and feel that duty has been done?

The school's system of care

Like most modern institutions, schools have developed into highly complex organisms. The main split is between the curriculum — the learning business — and what is called 'pastoral care'. In the old days schools were divided up into houses; now they are organised, more often, into 'year groups' and 'tutor groups', and in these groups personal welfare is the issue, rather than the learning subjects of the rest of school life. This organisation is a device to separate the caring business from the learning business. Sometimes there's a deputy head with specific responsibility for pastoral care, sometimes a 'school counsellor'. The counsellor is the school 'shrink', a kind and friendly soul who dabbles a bit in child psychology, mixes with the probation officers and social workers, and peddles help and advice rather than facts and skills. It's a fair bet that any teaching the school counsellor does will be in social education for the non-academics. It's clear from what they say that many teachers wonder whether this separation of care from learning is a good thing. After all, they *all* want to care and they are bound to develop special relationships with particular young people with whom they get along particularly well. That is the way of relationships, the way of the world.

One aspect of the care system is the part concerned with 'careers'. There may be a careers teacher in the school, who does nothing else but that. More often 'careers' is not a subject that's taught, it's just an office with lots of leaflets about the army and nursing. It's a place where the process of helping you 'make the right career choice' or 'occupational selection' begins. One girl commented:

'I hate school — I just hate it. I skip it. Sometimes I stay at home on my own. I wanted to go into hair-dressing.

Have you had careers lessons?
Yeah, but I skipped 'em all. I went to one, but it wasn't any help to me, it was just boring. Just a whole load of leaflets set out on a table, and that was it.'

And another girl said:

'The careers teacher gave me tests to find out what kind of jobs I'd be good at, and I came out well in art, and working with people, and then she gave me all these books to look through of all different kinds of jobs and that. I didn't fancy any of 'em.'

Naturally those whose career is marked 'more learning', at least to start with, will not need to be too bothered about this. The army and nursing apart, 'careers' are likely to be the portion of the academic child. The rest, besieged with advice about 'making the right career choice', are simply faced with the need to get a *job*. These are the young people who, because of the lack and inadequacy of work and work experience in schools will, in an ideal world, move from one job to another, to get that range of experience they never got at school. Now when it comes to talking about jobs, this isn't an ideal world, though we gather there are still opportunities in the army and nursing. That makes 'careers' an even more questionable activity. Can you fairly suggest to a child who will be lucky to get one offer of paid employment that he has any choice in the matter?

In our discussions with young people about 'careers lessons' and advice in schools, we found that, very often, the talk came back to *exams*. The two questions, careers and exams, seemed closely allied.

'If you hadn't fixed up a job, what would you have done? Has anyone in school talked to you about it?

The careers teacher isn't interested in the jobs round here, he just tells you about exams.'

This girl had found the same thing:

'In the careers lesson we had boxes of cards, and we had to read them and answer questions. They're all printed — they're called Signposts, I think.

Was that helpful?
It wasn't very helpful. It just explained what a nurse would have to do, and the exams you'd have to take to be a nurse, like you'd have to take all these exams and O levels and things and then go to university and train and everything. I didn't feel as keen as I was at first.'

Sometimes you can't win:

'I wanted to leave at Easter, and the headmaster said that they were going to chuck me out because I wasn't working for my exams. When he said that, I was really pleased, because I'd found a job and all. But when I told him that, he turned round and said they'd decided not to throw me out because it would worry my mum and dad.'

Learning and caring systems survive courtesy of two other systems. On the one hand there is control and discipline, on the other, responsibility. Control and discipline are the most important and they begin outside the school. The first control task is to enforce attendance, and this is enshrined in law. Generally parents act as agents for this control but sometimes their efforts, or lack of them, mean that other adults, known as Educational Welfare Officers, are brought in.

Within school the control task is to enforce the learning and childhood-prolongation processes. The idea is that if you don't like or cannot handle the kind of learning school has to offer, then you do not cause trouble to those who do and can. Control is achieved by grouping young people. Peculiarly, you are only treated as an individual when you do something wrong. It is also achieved through the development of a *dependent relationship* between young person and teacher, since fact-and-skill learning are the principal activity of the school. The child must rely on the teacher to get hold of this learning. The learning is the passport to success.

Responsibility systems in school amount simply to the giving out of peripheral functions to those who have shown the best signs of adjustment to the care and learning system.

3 Coping with Youth: Out of School

While the appearance of schools has often come to resemble the super-market rather than the corner shop, with both the size of the buildings and the range of learning products available increasing, the teacher/learner system probably has more in common with the charity than the corner shop. It is essentially a second-hand process, where the teacher is an intermediary rather than an expert. The fact that much of what is conveyed through the learning system is not from the horse's mouth, has a dulling effect on it. This can be demonstrated by the converse: the impact of first-hand information on young people, when it is demonstrated or conveyed by an enthusiast. Sometimes schools do bring in experts, or even go out to them, and whether it is a farmer shearing sheep, or an actor playing a part, there will usually be somebody among the group of young people who will be excited and motivated by what they see.

First-hand learning

It is when they are outside school that young people are most likely to come into contact with experts. By experts we mean people who actually do a job, and who have the skills about which children have learned at second-hand in schools. The first-hand experience can be of anything. Experts may be observed on the street or, more commonly, on the screen. It's not just because Steve Ovett and Brendan Foster won gold medals that young people wanted to sign up at tracks and clubs the next day. It's also because they are there, right before your very eyes, looking quite normal and displaying craft and expertise. When the athletes say it was hard work, work means something different from what the teacher says you should do if you're going to pass your exams.

The influence of out-of-school experts affects many aspects of young people's lives, they counter the influence of the second-hand school learning system, and provoke in schools a need to further enforce and control the dependent teacher-learner relationship. The system has to provide different forms of motivation to replace the primary form — seeing the expert and being enthused by the expert's enthusiasm, commitment and expertise. One way of providing secondary or 'fake' motivation is through systems of control or discipline, delivering punishment on one hand and reward on the other. Encouraging competitiveness also helps.

When you have been working as a school teacher for years, it is easy to feel that young people who have rejected school learning have rejected all learning. This is the danger, of course, and it does happen that the school experience destroys all curiosity, enthusiasm and motivation. But fortunately these are hardy plants, however little they are nurtured. Here is an example of a blossoming. The boy who talked to us is sixteen. He is due to leave school in a few weeks and he won't be sitting any exams at all:

'One of me brother's mates runs a fuel injection business. I asked him if he wanted a boy, just to help out, and he asked me to come up there. I went to have a look round and got to like it. He showed me what to do.

What exactly do you do?
Diesel engines have special pumps on them. An ordinary mechanic can service the engine, but this pump — it's only about eight inches square — it's sealed, it's got the firm's seal on it. Any fuel injection technician can undo the seal and work on it, but an ordinary mechanic can't. It's to make sure that it's not tampered with, because you can adjust it to pump the fuel in faster or slower. So I'm just dealing with these injectors. You know the spark plugs on a car? Well, on diesel they'll be fuel injectors. When the air is compressed and gets hot, it's at that moment that the fuel is injected and it explodes and pushes the piston down.

Did you find out about this at work?
Well, we did have motor mechanics at school and the teacher taught me something about it, but he doesn't know much about the commercial side of things — he's just the motor vehicle teacher. But there's teachers and teachers. The bloke I work for is a teacher, but he's a mate too.'

It's hard to convey how this young school leaver lit up when he was talking about fuel injection. First hand learning seems to have worked for him in several ways. His teachers felt that there was no chance of motivating him to work in school, and he had been in trouble continually for disobeying school rules.

Looking after yourself and making decisions

The responsibility systems among young people in school are strange. Of course, it's encouraging to remember that in schools, both primary and secondary, *some* young people, at least, are given responsibility. Earlier we talked about the 'functionless vacuum' which seemed the best way of describing the total system we have devised for dealing with youth through the prolongation of childhood. This is not just a *school* problem, school is just a part of the childhood extension business, albeit a big part. So it is encouraging to be able to say that there are responsibility systems in schools: prefects, monitors, the young people teachers know they can rely on to do things.

But to be given responsibility is one of the *rewards* given by schools for what the army used to call 'long service and good conduct'. That means that if you can show how well you can adjust to all aspects of the school system, then you can have a responsibility for delivering it in the future. More rarely you might even get a taste of administering and shaping it, but that doesn't happen much. As well as being a reward-system, responsibility in schools is task-oriented. The system requires certain jobs to be done and certain young people are selected to carry them out.

For every one waking hour young people spend within the school environment, they spend about three outside it. This takes account of holidays and weekends, but not the time they spend asleep. A lot depends on how old they are, but when you work the time out, it looks roughly like that. Where on earth does all the rest of this time go?

While the amount of time actually spent in school each day, each week, each year changes hardly at all between six and sixteen years, the distribution of the remainder of a young person's time does change. In particular the amount of time during which a young person *could* be responsible for his or her own life, or that segment of it, increases. The total time out-of-school increases too, because the young people in question will keep longer waking hours — if they want to.

There are two ways of looking at the non-schooled lives of young people. First of all the non-schooled period can be broken down into sections depending on who they are with and who they have contact with, directly or indirectly. Secondly, it can be examined in terms of what they are doing.

The 'who' analysis comes down to contact with young people,

family and 'others', usually adults. And, of course, being on their own; an oft-disregarded need of young people and all people. The 'what' analysis also comes down to three areas: being aimless, or just 'doing nothing', (we all 'do' this for part of our time); pursuing an interest for pleasure, self-satisfaction or improvement; and finally, meeting basic needs: natural functions, productive labour functions, economic functions (buying goods and services), and social functions. Social functions aren't just meeting people, they are being part of groups and communities.

Now if you check yourself off on these, whether you are young or old you may find the results come out like this: on the 'who' scale, young people come into direct contact with very few 'others', and we 'others' come into very little direct contact with young people; on the 'what' ratings it is clear that young people have no appreciable productive labour functions and thus no appreciable economic functions. Those social functions which require expenditure will be available only to those young people with some spending power. Even simple contact with 'others' may be difficult because it costs money to move. Those social functions which involve more than meeting and intercourse, which involve *role*, are almost completely absent.

So, even though the amount of time a young person has in which he or she could be responsible for his or her own life *increases* during the period of extended childhood, this time is not usually spent in extending contact with 'others' nor does it necessarily go to developing labour, economic and social functions. What actually happens to each individual depends on the strength and attractions of the family, on the one hand, and other young people on the other hand. The relative influence of these two forces depends on environment, too, because though you may want to be with your friends, it may cost money, money you don't have, to get to them.

The ability to realise your developing capacity for being in charge of your own life is not, then, always realised. Unless, of course, your family gives you money, or you can get some kind of part-time job to earn some. This tends to make the extension of a young person's horizons and relationships, the development of economic functions and social usefulness, a matter of privilege and chance.

Consider just what that adds up to. First we have a school system which isolates young people, as a group, from most people, other than teachers, and which enforces, as far as possible, their place as recipient learners. Beyond this school system they are part of a family and social system which tends towards immobility and limits the horizons of their contact with other people and the possibilities they may have to be useful, to have a function.

Youth clubs and organisations

The perfect example of these limited horizons and functions is the youth club. The provision of facilities for 'youth work' forms part of every local education authority's budget. It is a very small part indeed.

There are two kinds of youth work: youth *clubs* and youth *organisations*. Clubs are just buildings: places where young people can go, which will cost them little or nothing to go to. At worst they are places of cut-price, fifth-rate entertainment and diversion. Organisations seem to have a slightly stronger sense of purpose. They either have a more clearly defined set of activities on offer than generalised 'entertainment and diversion' and/or a more clearly defined method of working: offering uniforms, beliefs and being much more directive with the young people who join them.

The provision of entertainment and diversion approach, which is often call 'non-directive', will provide an informal forum for contact with other young people and with a few other adults, who are there to oversee the whole operation or to provide more specialised and expert services. The more directive approach makes contact with other young people secondary to the pursuit of an interest or the development of a skill, through contact with skilled, interested, experienced adults.

The directive approach takes for granted, and makes use of, the child-teacher relationship. It extends the curriculum. The non-directive approach tries to develop entirely different relationships between young people and adults. These are relationships which are not teacher-learner oriented either in disciplinary or curricular terms. If you ask non-directive youth workers to define what they're doing, they will probably call it 'informal social education'.

While it would be easy to say that the directive approach works because it uses, and probably reinforces, the dependent child-adult relationship developed by school, we cannot dismiss it as easily as that. Likewise, although much non-directive youth work often fails, both because it lacks clarity of purpose and, more important, because whatever we do the schooled young person continues to behave as a child, even when put in an entirely new environment, there are lessons in this approach, too.

What directive youth organisations and activities do provide is time and place for contact with experts and the pursuit of interests and talents, and opportunities for both of these are limited in the school setting. What the non-directive youth clubs offer is a chance for young people to develop relationships of a 'social' rather than dependent nature with adults, who try to listen and sympathise rather than bark and shout. The outcome may be disappointing, the background all too commonly the (oft derided) coke-and-table-tennis, but they do try, and for some young people it works.

There are features common to both approaches. Youth work is an area which relies on lay involvement. It has been estimated that something like 250,000 adults are involved in one form of youth work or another. The great majority of these people are either volunteers, or people who work for a couple of evenings a week over and above their normal jobs, for a few pounds a night. Paid volunteers, you could call them.

But both approaches are also essentially paternalist. They rest on the philosophical base that *we adults need to provide for the young people*. They share the view that young people are children who need to be played with, titillated, counselled and kept busy by us, and if the odd precocious one wins a gold medal at 14, then that's just wonderful.

The young people have no say in it at all — and if we offer them a chance to have a say, they never *have* anything to say for themselves. That's because they lack confidence, words, skills and experience to say it. Those abilities develop with youth, they are not skills which children possess. And they are not skills which we care to develop and encourage in our children. Because we decide that they need to be provided for. It is a vicious circle — a multi-million pound vicious circle.

Alternative responses to the needs of young people

There is one particular aspect of 'youth work' which deserves closer examination.

There are now organisations called 'youth action' or 'young volunteer' organisations. These provide for young people, just like the approaches we've already described, but what they provide cannot be called informal, non-directive recreation, and social education, nor is it formal, directive skill and interest learning and development. In many ways these organisations have taken the best of both approaches. They provide opportunities for community service.

The title conjures a mixture of unpalatable visions: of middle-class philanthropy by public school sixth formers; of less able school pupils being kept out of harm's way playing dominoes at the Derby and Joan club; of petty offenders repaying the community for the wrongs they've done by serving 'Community Service Orders'. It means all kinds of things to most of us, from sponsored walks to harvest festival food parcels.

Yet whatever its motivation, in spite of the way much of it is organised and regardless of some of the dubiously useful purposes to which it has been put, at the core of community service organisations there is something unique. A young person is *not* done unto by these organisations. True, community service at its worst may amount to the same task-oriented responsibility we've already seen in schools. True, it may amount to the performance of tasks which, allocated by adults steeped in the idea that these people are still children, are childlike in their demands and nature. True, it may mean that young people merely move from being pets to being slaves. But even when we acknowledge that there will be those kinds of practical outcome sometimes — and there are, all the time — we must repeat that there is something unique at the core of it all. There are plenty of examples around of what can result when the basic concept and those involved in it are not misused. These show that community service is not just an opportunity for not being done unto, but also an opportunity to break the grip of those whose multi-million pound business it is to prolong childhood.

It is not surprising that community service activity commands a low priority in schools as far as time, resources and who is considered suitable to do it are concerned. And it is not surprising that out-of-school young volunteer work commands a low priority in local authority provision for youth work.

The education service, like so many other parts of the public service system, is based on a single policy. In the education service this policy says that education means school up to the sixteenth year. The service also features the common tendency of all public services to meet a need with an institutional response as its main action. Although there are sometimes alternative actions incorporated in its response, it is the institution which dominates this response. This means that choice within the education service is very limited, because the system is based on the premise that the policy is good for everyone and that the policies within the policy —

academic study, learning only from teachers — are also good for everyone. So that alternatives are starved, and real choices — of different forms of educational environments which use the three forms of potential action, institutional, individual and collective, in different balances and with different purposes to suit the wide variety of needs among individuals — these choices are absent.

At the margins there are small signs of life. Alternatives gain toe-holds in education, in spite of the institutions which consume most of the resources available, resources of manpower and money. Often the institutions will grab workable alternatives, distort them and assign them to a very small place in their own practice. Alternative schools have often become 'truancy centres'.

In an account of one alternative education project, two organisers wrote about their reliance on local mothers to help run their project:

> 'The implicit belief that there are many people in the community who aren't qualified in any formal certificated sense . . . yet who have enthusiasm and ability for this sort of work, is fundamental to the operation of this project . . . local mothers . . . twenty years of child-raising makes them as qualified as any certificated teacher.'
> (David Brockington and Roger White, *In and Out of School*)

This project is helped with finance from the local statutory education service. These funds are necessary for survival, yet the receipt of them makes the project a part of the system that the young people they are dealing with have clearly rejected. The survival of such an experiment, alongside institutional provision, is hopeful.

There are others. And individual young people do take their own initiatives, getting advice and help and knowledge from other adults, not just those prescribed by the education service. They are small signs of life because many young people, totally dependent on the institutions, or alienated from them, steadily lose the ability to learn in a self-programmed way, even when they have escaped from the institution's net. It's alarming, but encouraging, too, when a seven-year-old asks 'Dad, what's a micro-processor?', because he's seen one, or heard somebody talk of one. It's much more alarming, and totally discouraging, when a fifteen-year-old cannot be bothered to ask.

What happens to young people when, for the first time, they have a choice?

4 The Change at Sixteen

Suddenly, at the age of sixteen, choices appear to unroll before young people. At this age they have three options open: to leave school and seek work; to leave school and continue in education, but in a 'college' rather than a school environment; to stay on at school.

The choices are not quite as clear-cut as that, and for some young people the eventual result will be a mixture. For those who stay on at school there are 'link courses', which amount to a mixture of school and college. And those who find work may well go to college for what is commonly called 'day-release' or, in some areas, 'Unified Vocational Preparation'. These choices are also not clear-cut for another reason. They may well not be made by young people on their own. Parents exert influence over these choices, and that can lead to conflict. And the young people themselves may be expressing a desire, and consequent choice, to get out of school. In many cases a desire to *get into work,* is, when examined, a desire to *get out of school.*

The National Child Development Study fills in some of the background to both those desires. In the study of sixteen year olds, what they wanted for themselves looked like this, in figures:

University/Polytechnic	12%
College of Education	5%
Technical/Commercial/Secretarial College	9%
Colleges of Art/Music/Drama	3%
Other full-time, further/higher education	4%
Uncertain	7%
None of the above	67%

(Ken Fogelman (ed), *Britain's Sixteen Year Olds.*)

That doesn't mean that all the 67% will leave school at sixteen, instead of staying until seventeen or eighteen, but most of them will. In fact, 62% told the researchers that they were most likely to leave at sixteen. The area of conflict with parents can be seen in the same study's finding that only 52% of parents expected their children to leave at sixteen.

Then there is the other issue: is leaving a positive choice or a negative one? Is it getting into something new, or just getting away from something old? On this question of 'why leave?' the study says:

'Several reasons could be given by each child and we cannot yet identify the overlap. Almost half (47%) said *they wanted to earn a wage and be independent as soon as they could*. 12% — and it seems likely that many of these replies will have been in conjunction with the above reason — said that *they needed to earn as soon as possible because their family needed the money.* 19% said that *they didn't like doing school work*, 4% *wanted to get married* in the next year or so, and 22% felt that among their important reasons for leaving was that *they were not good enough to stay on.'*

The reasons given for leaving are depressing, and suggest that a fairly large proportion of sixteen-year-olds don't like school and, even more depressing, realise that they are labelled 'unsuitable'.

Leave school or stay on?

What happens at sixteen, then, is a shake-up of the academic pecking order, and the result is predictable. Most of those who stay on at school have secured a good collection of GCE 'O' levels and a very good clutch of CSE passes. These become our 'academic' post-sixteen group. For the most part they will continue strictly academic studies in school. Another group will continue full-time education in colleges of further education, or similar institutions, which are *primarily* oriented towards *vocational* education. Vocational education is directed towards a specific 'calling', towards job related skills or qualifications, be they in brick laying or nursing. This group will be, for the most part, less 'academically able' and will have fewer GCE's or good CSE's. These are our 'vocational' post-sixteen group.

Then there's the rest who, as we've seen, considerably outnumber the other two groups. They are the group we are mostly concerned with. Up to now we have been talking about *all* young people, and although we are now focusing on one, albeit large, section of them, much of what we want to say has relevance to those who 'stay on' in one setting or another. When their turn comes to leave their problems are less acute, because they are older, and because they fit into the professional, managerial/administrative and skilled parts of the labour market reasonably easily, though we suppose we should mention the frustrations of those who find no room at the work-inn, even when they brandish a teacher's certificate or a degree. In a way, that may go to show how ill-informed their choices at sixteen were. Those who remain in the institution-dominated clutches are, when they finally leave, most likely to transfer themselves into very similar institutional clutches, simply swopping the role of client for that of professional master.

We should mention the exceptions to our general description of these three groups: open-access sixth-form colleges, or the non-vocational aspects of the work of colleges of further education, and so on. Some young people without much in the way of a first qualification, GCE or CSE, will stay on and try again, or try harder, either because they are afraid of making the break from school, because they still feel dependent on educational institutions, parental pressure, just plain indecision or putting off the inevitable. One of the young people who talked to us about this dilemma was a young Indian, who had left school at sixteen with CSE passes in maths and physics. This school leaver had taken a good deal of notice of his family's views and preferences:

'My father didn't know anything about apprenticeship or anything like that, he just thinks education is everything, so he said that I should go to college and get some 'O' levels. Well, after I did it I couldn't reach the standard to pass the test, and at the end of the year I had to leave after taking only one 'O' level. It was physics, and I failed it. My mum says she sent me to college to get better qualifications to look for a job, but it hasn't turned out that way. It was their mistake, but they didn't really know anything.'

This lost year made it impossible for the speaker to get the apprenticeship he feels would have suited him, and has also made him a year older than other young people looking for work. That is no advantage at all when you've no qualifications to show for it.

Many young people we talked to had been pressured into further education in this way. The pressure came from teachers as well as parents, and we have already illustrated how teachers use expressions like 'you could do better' and 'I'm disappointed in you', to make young people feel guilty about not staying in education. But some young people know that for them this would simply mean postponing the fateful day, that the qualifications they get won't mean much and that they might as well get out there and get on with it.

Another source of pressure and fear is the knowledge that unemployment among young people is growing. It is surprising how widely this is known among young people of thirteen years and over. They may not recognise a picture of the Prime Minister when it is shown to them, as a recent survey observed, but they do know that it's hard for school leavers to find jobs. The knowledge comes usually from seeing older brothers and sisters, other relatives and friends out of work. But teachers do discuss this as a problem, as well.

Colleges of further education and similar institutions are, in many places, bulging at the seams these days. In 1975/76, for example, 29,000 *more* 16-18 year-olds were in further education than in the previous year (183,000 compared to 154,000).

> 'The extent to which this buoyancy in the number of students in non-advanced further education is attributable to the high rate of youth unemployment is conjectural, since other factors have clearly been important. However, there is no doubt that the prospect of becoming unemployed must have been a dominant influence in many of the individual decisions to stay in full-time further education.' (*Young People and Work*, Manpower Services Commission)

It seems likely that unemployment causes some of those young people who would like to leave further education to stay on, even when they recognise that it is unsuitable for them, and they are unsuitable for it. Liverpool's education authority played on the fear of an outside world without enough jobs in it, with their 'Return and £earn' scheme. The title makes its point. This scheme, and others like it, have used an officially-discovered loophole which allows young people to go back to school for part of each week and still retain their entitlement to benefit payments from the state.

Bearing in mind the exceptions we've noted, let us compare the young people who leave with those who stay on at school. The MSC-sponsored surveys (*Young People and Work*) carried out in late 1976/early 1977 included one of a random sample of 3000 sixteen-to nineteen year olds. Some of them were still in educational institutions, some were at work, and some were unemployed. Of those staying on, at school or elsewhere, 45% had 5 GCE 'O' levels and above. Only 18% of the leavers in employment had this, and only 12% of those who were unemployed had this. Further, *one quarter* of those at work had no qualifications and one half of those unemployed had no qualifications.

This is predictable, but still astounding. Even if we measure 'success' on the school barometer, that academic scale which the school uses and, one assumes, judges itself by, then schools are doing an abysmal job. A large proportion of the young people they turn out are emerging with *nothing at all*.

From another angle, we can look at these young people in class terms. The MSC-sponsored survey of 3000 16-19 year olds showed that, of those staying on, at school or elsewhere, 58% came from families in the A, B and C1 social class brackets. Only 28% of those in employment were from those groups, and only 16% of those unemployed were from them. Further, 70% of those at work were from classes C2, D and E and a monstrous 80% of those unemployed were from these groups.

But it is not enough to look at young workers and work seekers in academic and class terms alone. They have other characteristics. To a large extent they are on their own. They may have some idea of what they want to do, of what kind of employment is available locally. But they don't have much idea of how to go about *getting it* or, for that matter, how to go about *doing it*. They will have a sense that they are failures, because they have failed at school. They will, in many cases, be lacking in self-confidence. And in the harsh and brutish world in which they now find themselves, the one thing they need is self-confidence. An instructor on a course for young unemployed people commented on the reaction of young people to leaving school:

'They think they are hard done by at school — they can't get out quick enough. But at school they have thirteen or fourteen weeks holiday — at work they'll be lucky to get three. They don't think of this before they leave school and it comes as a great shock to them. We find that kids come here reasonably enthusiastic, and after the first week they're shattered.'

Ways to get experience

Quite a large proportion of these young people will have had some experience, not necessarily of work, but of the 'world of work'. Before they reach sixteen young people get this experience in three ways: through part time or 'holiday' jobs, through school 'work experience' schemes, or through school community service programmes.

Rather more than half the young people reaching this age have had some kind of spare time job. For most this amounts to less that 9 hours a week, and their average earnings are £2-3. On the whole the work is not particularly satisfying — shelf-stacking in super-markets, for example. And it may be quite hard and exhausting, like delivering newspapers in all weathers. It is also not very well paid. Yet for some young people it is a useful experience and an early way into a future job. It can also prove a rare opportunity to feel a contributing part of a world which prefers children to be dependent, rather than responsible, as we have already seen.

There's potential in these sorts of jobs, for young people to feel that they are being useful and to have a role. But they have two painful drawbacks. Firstly, the conditions of work, and the number of hours that young people may work, are set down by local authorities, subject to certain conditions laid down in an Act of Parliament passed 45 years ago. This says that there should be no work for under 13s and that 13-16 year olds can only work in certain non-industrial settings for no more than 2 hours a day, and not before 6am or after 8pm. Other restrictions are laid down by local authorities.

Remember that school leaver, who talked about his job in the scrap-yard? Remember how he worked until 11.00pm one Saturday? Remember how much the job and the man he worked for meant to him? It was against the law for him to be working that late at night.

Just as we confuse young people by calling the 'study' that they do in school 'work', we confuse them further by the kinds of work we allow them access to as part-time workers. There are few jobs which rise above the level of drudgery in exchange for exploitive wages in certain, pretty limited, sectors. The legislation which imposes these limits harks back to the industrial revolution and the need to protect young children from harsh and dangerous working environments. But the need to protect still dominates our thinking about the young and work, even though the conditions which moved Lord Shaftesbury are not a common sight nowadays. So young people are prevented from any contact with jobs offering any dignity or satisfaction, jobs which might develop their confidence, maturity and responsibility. And the reasons are more than a century old. At present there is some pressure to use new legislation to prevent the financial exploitation of the young, because the poverty of Victorian industrialists hasn't completely disappeared in some areas and among some families. The effect of such legislation will make it more difficult for young people to find work, since it will further limit the hours and kinds of work that they can do. And if it pushes up minimum wages, they may well reach a point where Mum or even Dad will take the job instead.

The greatest irony is to come. It seems that those who remain at school after sixteen are more likely to have had spare time work experience than those who leave, and are considerably more likely to have had it than those who leave and find themselves unemployed. *(Manpower Studies 1978: Young People and Work,* HMSO). So the general rule seems to be that part-time work does not provide much in the way of dignity or satisfaction.

Only about one in ten young people find themselves involved in a school 'work experience' programme, and about one in four or five get experience through community service. Just as part-time work can mean exploitary drudgery, so work experience and community service can also be useless and unsatisfying. Work experience too often means standing behind someone else and watching *them* do the job. The excuses given by the organisers of such work experience are usually the insurance requirements: 'We'd be liable if she fell in the vat of boiling chocolate' or the legislation on child labour we have mentioned. So 'work' acquires a new meaning, work as *'watching'*. Community service can, also, and too often does, mean menial or peripheral social 'tasks', teacher or professional defined, limited by the same excuses as work experience. We show young people our social problems and allow them to play around them, as remote from the action as possible.

In our conversations with young people, Saturday jobs and work experience were the subjects they talked about most. None complained of *feeling* exploited, and there was strong evidence that the experience they had of work was influencing the choice they now had to make. For many of these young people there was not a lot of choice anyway, since they had no qualifications at all when they left school, but such as there was was being further limited by the work experience they had already. Is it a bad thing that a sixteen year old can pronounce with conviction that he wants to be a butcher? And when you ask why, he says it's because he's worked in the butchers on Saturdays? *Experience,* however limited, influences choice. Here are four young people talking about this:

'I used to have a Saturday job carrying bags of coal, because me Dad used to be a lorry driver for a coal firm and I used to shovel coal into the wagon. I'm looking for a job like that now, but nobody wants a girl for heavy work — they say I can't do it.'

'I was mad on trainee chef. I had a job in a restaurant when I was still at school, and I was mad on cheffing, I wanted to leave school and go straight into it. But I couldn't get a job.'

'I work in a paper shop on Saturdays. I just serve and keep the stock up. That's terrible, the stock. You have to check the price is right and everything. I used to make a mess of it, but I've got the hang of it now. There's only the woman who owns the shop and me there. She's over eighty but she still runs it. She's very dependent on me, so I couldn't have a Saturday off, or she'd be lost. I'm there from 9 until 12 and then 3 to 6.30. I can't say I love it, but I'll probably end up in a shop when I leave school, won't I?'

'Me Mum isn't a proper geriatric nurse, she does all different things — helps and baths and cooks and cleans. I go up to the house where she works nearly every night. I don't help her — I'm not allowed to, you see — but the matron there talks to me about the kind of job I can do when I leave school. And I talk to the old people. I like talking to them, and I feel sorry for them, in a way, because they've gone back to their childhood, haven't they? Me mates think it's a good idea. Because they always need nurses for old people, don't they?'

What employers look for

All this amounts to some kind of experience, however much each aspect is stripped of worth or meaning. Having some *experience* clearly helps a young person to get a job, although perhaps we should remember that employers rate qualities like 'willingness' to work, basic literacy and numeracy, good appearance, specific educational qualifications, as more important attributes in job-seekers than 'previous experience'; though presumably experience is some guide to 'willingness', whatever that may mean. The MSC-sponsored studies noted these remarks from employers as 'typical':

'Untidiness and their general attitude. If they are not polite and have this couldn't-care-less attitude when they come for interview, I just can't be bothered with them. Some of them don't even bother to talk properly.'

'Lack of enthusiasm: one detects a certain feeling that they are only half wanting the job. One also feels that with low retail wages they would prefer to be on the dole.'

'I have them coming in with dirty fingernails, untidy hair, tatty dress, which shows what their general attitude to work would be.' *(Manpower Studies 1978, Young People and Work,* surveys of employers)

Other 'typical' comments we have come across focus on the irresponsibility of many young school leavers. This is held against them, not against the system which has induced it. This man, working with unemployed young people, made a most interesting comment:

'They have no responsibility for anyone else. I often wonder if, at the back of their minds, knowing that they are not yet eighteen, they don't altogether accept that they are completely responsible for themselves.'

An earlier study, carried out in 1972 *(Unqualified, Untrained and Unemployed,* HMSO) noted that most employers looked for personality, alertness and other personal qualities rather than paper qualifications, especially when they were recruiting for unskilled jobs. So the very things which young people have had as their principal enforced activities, academic studies, turn out to be not so useful, after all. At best, these academic qualifications may serve as a rough and ready guide to basic educational ability in literacy and numeracy.

This substantial difference in the requirements of industry and the products of school is hardly reassuring to the sixteen year old leaver. But the failure to get academic qualifications tends to lead to a lack in personal confidence and self-esteem which makes the young people unable to meet the *other* requirements of employers; enthusiasm, articulation and pride in appearance. Only for those at apprentice level and above do the paper qualifications count. But it does appear that as unemployment among the young increases, firms become more selective. So, increasingly, they look for the magic papers.

One girl we spoke to felt that it was not just the papers you brought, it was the papers you had to fill in when you got there, that were important:

'I don't agree with having to fill in all these forms for a job. They take the way you work from what you've written on a form. I think you should be tested on the work you're going to do — have a machine where you can have a go, then they can look at the work you've actually done. If I go for a job I like to tell 'em what I do, so they get the idea that I *can* work. If you've got to write it on a piece of paper, I'd take too long. I'd take something like two lines and it don't look very good. I prefer to tell people, or show 'em.'

Perhaps the most frustrating, galling and unintelligible thing to many young people looking for jobs is an *age* requirement. Some find that they are too old for apprenticeships, yet too young for jobs, or for the 'adult' oriented training schemes, called 'Training Opportunities', or TOPS for short, run by the MSC. A young man, presently unemployed, and his mother talked about some of the frustrations:

Mother: 'You see, this hospital business has really got me, because he was really liking it, and he's either too old or he's too young. These places need so much help that when young people are at school they get them to do it voluntary, but when they grow up and they leave school, they don't want them. It's not fair, really, because there's plenty of people that want help.

Son: Yeah, and I've been up the hospital and filled up application forms and that, but they just say 'Wait for a vacancy'. I've been up the hospital where I worked from school and they suggested taking up male nursing or being an orderly and that, but again you've got to go on a course and that, when you're a certain age. That's 19.

You've been unemployed since you had a construction job — four months. Have you tried for any other jobs?

Son: There's nothing else to do all day except look for jobs. Yesterday I phoned up a garage — I went for an interview there last week — and that had gone. They'd taken an older man on. It makes me laugh. You go for a voluntary job with old people, you'll probably get it just like that. But if you go to be paid — you're too young. The leader of our youth club said that me and me friend could go on a leadership course and be on the staff in the club. He said we can do that when we're nineteen.'

And it also appears that you can be *too* qualified for a job. A man who works with unemployed young people in an informal 'drop-in' centre, told us:

'There is a girl here, she has 9 O levels. She wants to work in personnel. So I sent her to a particular place where they wanted somebody to work in personnel. They told her, "You are over-qualified". Dammit — somebody goes to school to learn as much as possible, they need work that requires qualification — they tell her she is over-qualified. I said to her, "Next time you apply for a job, don't write it all down." She's now got a job as a pay-clerk.'

It is the comments of employers which form the practical bases of new provision for the young unemployed. The idea is to help them find work. The recent 'special' Youth Opportunities Programme, costing around £200 millions a year and expected to benefit just short of a quarter of a million young unemployed people per year has, as its objective, the idea of improving young people's *employability*. In other words this programme aims to provide the basic skills and experience which many young people lack, the skills, attitudes and experience which employers look for. And it also aims to improve the ability of young people to actually *get* jobs. A new set of phrases has emerged to cover both the doing and the getting aspects of employability: 'transferable skills', 'adaptive re-training', 'coping skills', 'life and social skills', 'job-search skills', etc. Together they amount to the 'skills of employability'.

It is hard to dispute or disagree with the aim of making unemployed young people employable when it is seen within the whole area of school-to-work 'transition'. As we have already explained, in the first part of this book, it is within this context that the problem is generally seen. We must admit to our own involvement in the processes of debate which led to this new programme, even to being in on the design and implementation of it. But is the government spending £200 millions a year on a repair job? And a rushed and inadequate repair job, at that? This job is being carried out on a group of young people, on whom others have already spent thousands of millions, and have caused the very failings which the new 'special' programme aims to repair. This is a good example of the self-perpetuating tendencies of public services in general, the youth services in particular. New institutions are erected to deal with the waste products of others.

What's so important about *work?* By work we mean what work eventually amounts to for many of the sixteen year olds who find it. That is, carrying out a task for 48 or 50 weeks a year, a task which very often has no apparent usefulness, inherent satisfaction or dignity. The purpose of doing it is simply to earn money to survive, and if the money is sufficient, to escape from work for the other 2 to 4 weeks of the year, and when each day's work is done. And when the worker sits down to think about what he's doing, it seems to be merely the creation of profit for people who do little or nothing.

In the wider perspective, then, what finding work amounts to for those young people who do find it, is simply a move from being an anonymous youth in an amorphous youth business to being an anonymous young worker in an amorphous work-business. This is *particularly* true for those who leave with nothing to show for the previous eleven years, and they expect it to be true. Their parents, teachers, adults they pass in the street, exemplify it. Work can be drudgery — yes, even for teachers and administrators — especially for school-failures. Why put on a big performance to obtain a job you don't really fancy? Employers complain about lack of enthusiasm among the young people they interview — but what do these kids have to be enthusiastic about? This young man went to a mill for a job as a welder:

> 'They said "Sweep up this, and put all that in the dustbin". There were large waste containers I had to dump. I once did some welding on a gate, but then they took me off it and told me to do cleaning again — I got very bored. They weren't helping me at all.'

He left it, and he's been unemployed ever since.

Job satisfaction

Pity the poor youth, then, as he discovers he's still just a nobody, a small part of somebody else's grand design.

> 'Consider a likely, useful job. A youth who is alert and willing but not "verbally intelligent" — perhaps he has quit high school as soon as he reasonably could — chooses for auto mechanic. That's a good job, familiar to him, he often watched them as a kid. It's careful and dirty at the same time. In a small garage it's sociable . . . you please people in trouble by fixing their cars, and a man is proud to see rolling out on its own the car that limped in behind the tow truck. The pay is as good as the next fellow's, who is respected.' (Paul Goodman, *Growing up Absurd*)

Confirmation that this sort of job, with those ingredients, is attractive, came from the school leaver we have quoted already, the one who has a job waiting for him in a scrap-yard. He described what gave him confidence and satisfaction:

> 'I like it when somebody comes up and says their motor's

knackered and would I have a look to see what's up with it. One Sunday I was coming back from the car-breakers with me brother and we saw this bloke with his bonnet up. I stopped and said "What's up?" and he says, "It just won't start." I says "Turn it over" and it weren't firing. So I looked at his petrol gauge and it were on full. I says "When did you set off?", he says "An hour ago." I says "Did you have a full tank then?" He says, "Yeah". I says, "If you'd been driving an hour your gauge would have gone down, wouldn't it?" So I undid the petrol pipe and he's turning it over, and there's no petrol there. The gauge was shorting out. He wanted to give me a fiver, but I said I didn't want it. We towed him to the petrol station and he made us take it then, just for doing that'.

That anecdote shows what 'job satisfaction' means to an unqualified sixteen year old. It's something that makes him feel somebody. But can that experience be sustained by the mechanic's job just described? Paul Goodman continues:

'So our young man takes this first-rate job. But what when he learns that the cars have a built-in obsolescence, that the manufacturers do not want them to be repaired or repairable? . . . Gone are the days of keeping the jalopies in good shape, the artist work of a proud mechanic . . . It is hard for the young man now to maintain his feelings of justification, sociability, serviceability. It is not surprising if he quickly becomes cynical and time-serving, interested in a fast buck.'

From school that is pointless, to work that is pointless. That's all the famous transition amounts to for many young people.

Disillusion: working in a factory

A study of over 200 young people working in a large factory, carried out from late 1975 to early 1977, provides some excellent, detailed analyses and observations on young people's experiences and attitudes in the early years at work. (Martin Simon, *Youth into Industry*). These 200 young people were mostly *boys,* and roughly half of them were *apprentices.* The apprentices were of two kinds: *technician* apprentices who have fairly good academic qualifications, and who have a substantial element of college and training-school further education and study inter-mixed with their on-the-job apprentice-learning; and *craft* apprentices, who are less well qualified academically and who become *craftsmen.* The other half of the 200 were *operatives*. This is another euphemism that has crept into the vocabulary, replacing blunter expressions like manual workers, or labourers. These operatives have few or no academic qualifications. Some of them may do day-release for some kind of basic non-academic examination, like 'basic engineering', while others will simply learn, on the job, how to use simple engineering tools.

The study shows declining satisfaction with the job as a whole for both operatives and apprentices, during the first four years at work. After that, satisfaction ratings improved. The study details this very carefully, by looking at the various aspects of work which comprise 'the job as a whole'. We thought we'd just take out two of these aspects: *the work itself* and *relationships with supervisors*.

For the apprentices, much of the first year at 'work' is actually spent in the factory's training school:

> 'Commenting on the actual jobs done in the training school . . . apprentices were more concerned with seeing the *need* for each task or series of tasks, and recognising the value of the knowledge and experience gained . . . There was some dissatisfaction expressed . . . about the fact that they machined a lot of components that were of little use and often scrap, and enthusiasm about the occasions that they had made something of value. (However) they understood that their level of skill was probably not sufficient to be engaged on production work of any value.'

For these young men this 'school' is a step on the transitional way, and it seems to have some of the charactistics of the old place. But after a year comes much more 'real' work on the job; for a while all seems well, but then:

> 'During the third and fourth years less satisfaction is apparent . . . the routine of work is becoming a disliked factor . . . and issues such as the way work is allocated to them are beginning to arise. Comments such as "I seem to get a lot of the odd jobs" are more typical . . . "I got fed up sitting around all day — really we're a pain in the neck (to the supervision)." These comments . . . reflect what appears to be a continuing problem in industry: that of how to give young people an interesting and useful training within the confines of production-orientated departments. There is a reticence on the part of some supervisors to give apprentices the more challenging work, and symptoms still remain of the opinion that apprentices are simply an "extra pair of hands".'

And how are the operatives doing?

'Comments that accompanied expressions of satisfaction suggest
that the newness or unfamiliarity of work is an important factor:
. . . "it's something new" . . . "it's not too bad at all". As the job
settles into a routine, satisfaction tends to continue until after
about 9 months to a year's service . . . As with apprentices there
were complaints that being young "you tend to get the odd (or
dirty) jobs" . . . routine was disliked by nearly a third of the total
sample, e.g. "I'm not sure I fancy doing this for ever" from a
young operative in a Press Shop full of repetitive jobs.'

But there is something else about the operatives:

'. . . many . . . did not *expect* to be satisfied with the actual work
. . . a common comment was of the nature "I don't really like this
job, but I didn't expect anything different" . . . one nineteen-
year-old described "a long slog each day".'

For some of these young people things change. For others, the long
slog each day is acceptable, perhaps with some resignation, as a
seemingly necessary part of life. After the first four years the
apprentice group:

'shows a rise in satisfaction with the work itself. The main reason
was clearly the successful completion of their apprenticeships,
leading into desired areas of work, new status and some new
responsibilities. Those dissatisfied were those disliking what had
become a "routine for life".'

For the operatives, such new areas, status and responsibilities are
quite naturally harder to come by:

'many operatives . . . do not expect to like their work; indeed, the
concept of "liking" work was alien.'

These young people, then, have low expectations of work and these
seem to be amply confirmed by their subsequent experience of it.
Social clubs and sports facilities may sweeten the pill. But for the
young people who leave school and expect to be treated like adults
when they enter work, it's a bit of a shock to find that they're not.
Others, wiser and reflecting maturely on their prospects, resign
themselves in an expectation of an indefinite future of routine.
A fortunate few find demands, satisfaction and dignity from work.

An interesting area is their relationships with supervising adults
during these early years. The operatives, as one might expect, make

more unfavourable comments about the quality of supervision and relationships than the apprentices. *How* you are treated has to do with your social, informal contact with the adults you work with and for, with the kinds of work those adults give you, with the expressions of support, reward and praise you get, with the help and advice you are offered: with how far you are treated as an adult. All this has a major effect on your satisfaction with the job.

We discussed this with young people before they left school. Many had complained of being tired of school 'because people tell you what to do'. But, we suggested, people will tell you what to do when you're working, too:

> 'I don't think so — they show yer. At least when you're at work you're responsible to one person. At school they're *all* leaning on you. And in school there's problems of favouritism — school isn't really fair. They don't give you a chance — they tell you to do something and expect you to know how to do it right away.'

That fifteen-year-old was sure it would be different when she left. The next young speaker left school two years ago and has had a succession of jobs he hated interspersed with periods on the dole. He admits to leaving jobs because, as his mother says; 'he doesn't want people over him, telling him'. When we suggested to him that this was inevitably going to be so, he said:

> 'Fair enough, you're told what to do once. But some jobs they keep on and on to you. And when people have got quick tempers, you sort of can't put up with it, really. Say if you're working somewhere and they have a go at you, and keep onto you in front of other people, other work-mates, they make you look small, you know.'

His father said:

> 'He doesn't like to be *told* to do a thing, but it's all right if he's *asked* to do a thing.'

And his mother said:

> 'I understand that reason, but the fact is, you can't always be asked, can you?'

And the consequence was that this nineteen-year-old stayed out of work with his parents worried stiff about him, as he got more restless, more bored.

The pity of it is that for many young people the early years at work provide the first, or at least the major first opportunity for direct relationships, social and learning, with adults *other* than teachers, parents and the odd aunt or youth worker. It seems that these relationships don't always work out:

> 'Young people who are in general expecting to be treated as an adult and appreciated on starting work, can find themselves in a situation with little social communication but a lot of ordering about, little interest shown in them but a lot of discipline imposed. They react against such authoritarianism in a number of ways, e.g. by answering back, muttering or staying silent, by generally pursuing a line of minimum cooperation: or by applying for a transfer or leaving. Unfortunately these styles of response may encourage such supervisors to continue their approach on the grounds that 'young people today are not what they used to be'. However, there is *no other way* for the youngsters to respond: they would be likely to receive short shrift from whatever more senior manager they approached . . . young people . . . who spoke of feeling like "a cog in the wheel", or said "we're just told to do something and we do it" are expressing an attitude that they are people in their own right . . . One young operative summed up the feelings of many when he said "I wouldn't put myself out for him" . . . ' *(Youth Into Industry)*.

These observations are confined to manufacturing industry, where the intrinsic interest and apparent worth of the work *itself* are, we suspect, most likely to be rather low. But as far as the question of relationships with adults is concerned, it seems fair to generalise from this evidence, since two types of industry form the main areas of employment for young people. One of them is distribution, transport and communication. The other? Manufacturing industry.

We shouldn't forget that most young people do get work by the Christmas after they leave school, though such a statement conceals a lot about particular problems in areas like Merseyside, Strathclyde and, believe it or not, Cornwall. It also conceals the fact — which is probably obvious anyway — that those with little to show for their eleven years at school are more likely to suffer longer periods of unemployment. The major similarity between new work and old school is that it can be just as suffocating, undignified and unsatisfying. Is this recent set of 'special provisions', to find employment opportunities for young people, a New Deal or a Three-Card Trick? What kind of jobs will be available to young people in the future?

5 Other Changes at Work

Until the first part of the 1980s more and more young people will be leaving school and looking for work each year than the previous year, as the 'bulge' which pre-occupied primary and secondary schools successively in the '60s and '70s finally reaches the end of the institutional road. And, just as now, a large proportion of them will continue to be rendered unfit for work and unprepared for finding it and coping with the boredom of much of it, by the experience and education gained during the first sixteen years of their lives. Can we really present *work* as something important to these young people, when we think of the areas of work into which most of them will go?

On the jobs side, what will be available in future looks even more depressing. The kinds of skills, knowledge and experience required in jobs has increased steadily as scientific and technological advantages have achieved industrial application. That is the fabled 'technological revolution' leading, so they say, to a 'post-industrial society' in which only one-tenth of the present work-force will be required, and able to produce all the food and material goods we need. It will, some say, be a change as great as that which has happened in agriculture. Three hundred years ago over 90% of the labour force was engaged in farming. Now the figure is around 2%. Since we have to import food, that figure may be artificially low; but in the United States, only 3½% of the labour force work in agriculture, and the country is a net exporter of food.

Parallel processes of technical and technological change are affecting our industrial workforce. Investment no longer simply creates jobs, as it used to. It may well destroy them, or, at best, where the investment produces 'new' industry, it will create very few jobs indeed. In the petro-chemical industry, for example, the investment of hundreds of millions in new plants has created only a few hundred extra jobs. In the 'old' industries, from glass-making through textiles, and even transport, new investment frequently causes what is termed 'labour-shedding' — there are fewer jobs than before. And, we are told, if we don't do it, we will become, as a nation, *less competitive*.

The overall effect, in a number of sectors of industry, is fewer jobs and the need, in those jobs that do remain, for higher skills. At the same time this process of technological change has created some truly moronic jobs. The designers, maintainers and repairers of the new machines may need higher technical skills, but the machine-minders and operatives need to know nothing, like the girl at the supermarket check-out.

No thought, no creativity, no personal relationship is required in these jobs. So we seem determined to nurture a technology superior to ourselves, without considering the ultimate conclusion: that many of us will become obsolete under its sway.

The trend towards fewer jobs with higher skill requirements, plus unskilled, unthinking jobs, means, among other things, that the traditional craft-apprentice-type jobs for young people are disappearing. The technician-apprentice jobs are becoming more important, and, as we have already said, these require higher qualifications for entry. What is happening is a growing mismatch between the kinds of jobs available to young people, and the kinds of young people looking for them.

The second feature of an economy with fewer jobs on offer is that there is a tendency for young people, like other workers, to settle for *less* than they would have done in previous years. Next time you go to the bank, ask the manager about the young people who start work in his branch. We guarantee he will say that they have better paper qualifications than young people starting in banks used to have. This isn't because schools are doing so much better in the way of examination results, it's because of the settling-for-less syndrome among reasonably well-qualified young people. This increases the pressure on the less qualified and makes the qualified feel cheated:

'There's so many people telling them to get the qualifications so as they'll get jobs easier . . . They are encouraging too many people to get the qualifications, and in the end there's not enough jobs left for them. You find that the people with all the qualifications aren't prepared to do hard graft — they think they're above it.'

We are told that the main 'job-loss' areas in the near future are likely to be in transport and communication, public utilities, agriculture (more!) and textiles. When you consider the geographical distribution of these it is plain that those areas which already suffer relatively high levels of unemployment, areas like the North-West and Scotland, are likely to suffer even more from these projected job losses. And it seems that more men are likely to be affected than women. And the list includes the distribution area — a key one for young unqualified people to find work in.

It is often observed that young people are forced to compete more and more with adults, as 'young people only' jobs become scarcer. And the adults they are competing with most particularly are married women, who return to work once their children go to school. In fact, it is estimated that the difference between 'registered' and 'unregistered' unemployment figures may be as much as 0.6 million, and that this is mostly due to married women who are 'unemployed' but not actually registered as seeking work. That is, unemployment may be over 2 million already, rather than the 1.4 million 'registered unemployed' we talk about at present. Now the MSC tell us that more and more married women will be seeking work, and that they will form an increasing percentage of the labour force as compared to men and young people. Put that alongside the 'sex' effects of the job losses mentioned above, and things look grim. It means that the size of the competition in the married women versus young people game is increasing. And we know that the married woman is more mature, more experienced, and probably more 'willing' than the young person.

True, the MSC predict that there will be some sectors of employment in which we'll see 'job gains'. These will be in 'professional and miscellaneous services', for example, and (perhaps) in the construction industry. *But,* and it's a big but, both of these are very dependent on government policy towards public service spending, and in the professional services area we have seen how an increase in public spending tends to result in new forms of institutional action, which exclude the lay and unqualified worker. Economic upturn will also, apparently, create 'small' gains in the manufacturing sector.

There used to be a good deal of argument about whether unemployment among young people is a *structural* or a cyclical phenomenon, which really amounts to an argument about whether what one *does* about it should be *permanent* or *temporary.* It seems now to be widely accepted that the problem is indeed structural, for all the reasons outlined in the previous pages. It is also accepted that societies making the leap into the new technological age are also making a leap into an age where mass unemployment will be a phenomenon which is not just confined to the young. It will take us a long time to adjust to that. One of the things that makes it a difficult concept to adjust to is the great gulf between the futurist view, of mass unemployment before the end of the century, or the 'leisured' society, and the short and medium term problems of today, tomorrow and the next decade or so. There is a problem of adjusting goals and objectives.

When we talk about the problems faced by young people when they reach sixteen, people say 'All this gloom and doom is one thing, but it ignores the fact that three-quarters of the young people who leave school each summer have found a job by Christmas.' That seems like a short-term goal three-quarters met. But it ignores something itself — the mindless and poorly rewarded nature of the jobs they are getting. Is this a desirable goal for the young people themselves? And what about the detail of the problem?

So far we've been talking in general terms about young people and those, in particular, who have few, if any, qualifications. There are two points of detail to spell out. First, unemployment among young people is not evenly spread throughout the country — a pretty obvious conclusion for most people. In some parts, like Merseyside, the figures for youth unemployment are very high, and many young people are unemployed for very long periods of time. Make them as 'willing', competitive and employable as you like, through schemes such as the MSC special programmes, and all you are doing is pointlessly, and perhaps unkindly, raising their expectations.

Secondly, certain groups of young people suffer disproportionately. Unemployment among girls has risen faster than unemployment among boys. Unemployment among young blacks aged 16 and 17 *trebled* between early 1973 and early 1977. It's not just the academically disadvantaged who suffer most. The young disabled person, the young offender or ex-offender, and the young educationally subnormal, also get a pretty low proportion of the jobs that are available.

We can think of this phenomenon of youth unemployment as a cancer, well established already in some areas, among some groups of young people, with its secondary growth reaching up and out to other, presently not-so-badly affected groups. It feeds eagerly on industrial and economic decay, on technological change, and on victims displaced by other entrants into the work force.

A programme of action is needed to tackle the cancer.

6 Self-Interest

A programme of action needs to respond to long term changes in the nature and availability of work, far beyond the present state of affairs. It cannot be limited by self-interest, nor should it take the form of a set of provisions based on institutions, whether these are existing institutions or ones created for the purpose. The school-leaving age might be raised to eighteen, for example, but as a programme of action against youth unemployment, that falls into all the traps.

Responses to our national problem are dominated by self-interest. While recognising the problem exists, the most we can do is demand 'government measures', unless we are part of the youth industry, that is, when we ask for 'more money to solve the problem'. At the other extreme (for such demands are most likely to be heard only by the political left and centre) the political right will insist on as little interference as possible. There is, in other words, a great void between institutional action and no action at all. That is alarming to us, and we think, to many others. The same responses are made to arguments about the need for a dignified and useful role for the young. It's always somebody else who should be doing something about it, unless you're a professional in the youth business. Then you're looking for ways to take over any new provision.

The Silver Jubilee Appeal was a good example of how this works in practice. The aim was to collect a lot of money from the public to 'help youth to help others'. Millions of pounds were collected, a good deal by young people themselves. Some was invested to provide funds for a permanent trust, the rest was handed out in grants right away. But when you look at where the money went, it's clear that by no means all, or even most, of it went to 'help young people help others'. The organisations which provide for youth saw that these money-raising activities would siphon funds away from their traditional sources. So they got themselves thoroughly involved in the organisational arrangements of the scheme. When the time came for grants to be apportioned, via the Lord Lieutenants in the counties, whose knowledge of young people was slim, it was these organisations who laughed all the way to the bank. Smaller schemes, run by young people, encouraging them to make their own decisions and seek out roles for themselves, were just as broke as ever. When we questioned this, we were told that young people could not be trusted to manage the money themselves.

In industry, too, it is self-interest which predominates. It is true that the CBI and the TUC both endorsed the government's decision to spend hundreds of millions of pounds on helping the young unemployed through the special programmes of the MSC. But that wasn't a difficult endorsement to give, so long as the bosses could say 'it doesn't cost me anything', and so long as the workers could say 'it's not going to interfere with my job in any way'.

The TUC passes resolutions about the 'obscenity of unemployment', the need to return to full employment and to have more government measures to help the unemployed. But these demands are based on this thinking: legislate, provide institutional frameworks. Don't ask more of us than that. Because our pre-occupations are with relativities, slipping behind in the pay race. We are busy protecting ourselves by preserving over-manning or by making change acceptable when it is 'natural wastage' or a productivity deal. We need our overtime. We may call for increased help for the elderly, that's a concern with other people. But in a way it's not, because we're all going to be pensioners one day, aren't we? We'll never be young again.

Where there's profit to be made, it's a similar story. Employers and shareholders are also governed by self-interest. Of course, social responsibility is good for PR, but as for the suggestion that profits might pay for help to the disadvantaged . . . we pay our taxes, don't we? And our profits are already punitively taxed, blunting our competitive drive, and anyway, the workforce has its beady eye on our profits already, they've just put in a claim . . . of course, we do second staff to help charitable organisations sometimes, through the Action Resource Centre which IBM set up for PR purposes. (We can off-load some of our lower calibre, nearing-retirement excess staff, and draw some good notices for it). And there's a little trust we've set up which hands out the odd grant. And we do work on local committees — we do our bit.

Self-interest finds expression in other ways. From the workers' point of view schemes of job creation and work experience for young people are tolerable *provided they do not interfere with the rights of paid workers.* In various parts of the country such schemes have been 'blacked' by local union branches, because such interference is anticipated. And what is offered to the young people in these schemes must be *work experience* and not actually *work*, because if it's the latter, that would certainly mean doing a job somebody else might think was theirs, or a job which somebody should be properly appointed to do. If the appointment to that job is made competitive, of course, it's unlikely that the young applicant will get a look in.

Employment protection legislation has not helped. Do employed workers care that it causes employers to think twice before taking on the unknown quantity represented by a young and inexperienced worker? This legislation protects existing workers, but ignores those who haven't got that privileged status and it provides employers with a cast-iron excuse to pass over the young applicant.

It isn't only legislation which has this consequence. The very availability of government funds can lead to it also. For example, the MSC's Youth Opportunities Programme makes funds available to employers who are prepared to take on a young, unemployed person and give them up to six months' work experience. In 1978 the MSC produced statistics which showed that over 80% of these young people were, following or even during the period, finding permanent work, very often in the firm which sponsored the work experience scheme. That's impressive, but who were the young people offered the opportunities in the first place? Did employers look for the best raw material available, or did they look for those most in need? The answer is that usually they looked for the best, with a few significant 'socially responsible' exceptions. The second question is harder. Are some employers using 'work experience' as a way of paying for recruitment policies and practices which they would have operated anyway? This seems to happen in some cases. And that goes beyond self-interest and becomes unscrupulous. But can it be stopped, and how? If there are more stringent rules governing these work experience opportunities, then fewer firms will offer them. If an army of inspectors goes round to check on practices, then money will be spent on new bureaucracies rather than the problem itself — young people without work.

Another kind of self-interest works against the development of rules and regulations, and that is political self-interest. This seeks to show that the numbers of unemployed people are declining. *How* doesn't matter all that much. What is important is that the dole queue is visibly shorter, even if that means turning a blind eye to the self-interest of those who are helping to shorten it.

All these self-interests are hidden beneath caring and concerned resolutions and caring and concerned institutions. But there is one group, who, while not really promoting their own interests, are guilty of passing by on the other side. This is the group of young people who do well out of the education system, remaining at school after sixteen and progressing to some institution of higher education. It is true that they have more problems than they used to when they emerge from these institutions, because the demand for their services, too, is not up to the level of supply. But while they are students, are they expressing any concern for the less-privileged young? It doesn't seem so. In many colleges some students take part in Student Community Action, trying to get involved with local communities, sometimes penetrating professional barriers to stimulate self-help projects catering for community needs. But that is a *small* movement, and the students who are not part of it say that it is a vestige of Victorian philanthropy and an undesirable substitute for jobs which ought to be done by the modern welfare state. Those were the kinds of views which caused the National Union of Students, after a flirtation with this movement, to divest itself of Student Community Action. Thankfully the people involved found other sources of money to keep a national focus alive.

Students, too, care enough to do their annual resolution passing, and, like everybody, to demand government efforts. But what if cuts were made in the current vast expenditure on higher education, to stimulate work for the disadvantaged young school leaver? What if students were required to be involved in a practical way with disadvantaged groups — as they are in Indonesia, Nepal and Nigeria? It seems that the *rights* of students, like those of workers, profit-makers and the rest, are to be preserved, whatever measures are taken for young and unemployed people. We wonder if any measures can have any impact in the face of such narrow interests and such self-absorption.

7   Continuing Education

The young people who leave school at sixteen do not necessarily sever their contact with education. Some will go on full-time courses at Colleges of Further Education or 'open-access' sixth form colleges. This can be difficult for them, for the grants are mostly meagre. Other young people will retain, for a time, some part-time contact with these Colleges by various means: day release, whereby their employers allow them, or ask them, to take courses of study; 'Unified Vocational Preparation' (UVP) (on which we will elaborate); 'Return and £earn', using the benefit loophole to allow continuing education for the young unemployed. In addition, some employers have 'Training Schools' on their own premises, where young employees — especially but not solely apprentices — spend some time when they start work. Many industrial sectors have an Industrial Training Board to advise and help with all these aspects of continuing education.

Through any of these various means, then, some young people will keep in contact with the *formal* educational institutions for some time. Indeed, well-respected individuals, such as Professor Stonier of Bradford University, argue that, in the light of the changes occurring in the world of work, the best option open to young people is to remain in education and find a place, by that route, in the 'knowledge industry'. Professor Stonier argues that this will be, in the future, the wealth creating base. That may be so, but will there be a place in it for everybody?

But continuing education, and the practice and potential of it, is not by any means confined to such formal, structured contact with institutions. Some young people will remain, post-sixteen, in contact with the youth service, which does not offer the formal academic or vocational education that the colleges offer, but *informal* education (as youth workers call it), or plain informality, (as many young people say).

Secondly, some young people will continue their education by enrolling in adult education classes, if they can afford it. For many the aim will be the renewal of the pursuit of an elusive 'O' or 'A' level that they didn't manage to get at school, for others the more

leisurely pursuit of some non-vocational, plain 'interesting' or diverting class in DIY or pottery or whatever.

Thirdly — and this is the major growth area — there are those who, unemployed and finding a place in the Youth Opportunities Programme, will be called 'trainees'. The fact that they are paid an *allowance* rather than a *wage* means that they should spend part of their time studying, formally or informally or both ways, rather than working or work experiencing.

Fourthly, the education of many young people continues almost un-noticed, through their contact in work, social and other environments with other people, non-professional or 'lay' people.

A description of the ways in which these various means of continuing formal or informal education operate, or might operate, will occupy some of the rest of this book. Sometimes these means are related, sometimes they are fragmented, sometimes in conflict, sometimes harmonious. Since 'advice', as opposed to instruction, is an important part of the continuing education of young people, we shall examine that, too.

Here we want to pick out some features of the formal institutions of continuing education, the ones that come under the heading 'further education', and the effects which programmes for the unemployed are having on them. We shall look at the more informal opportunities for continuing education later.

A chance missed

The 1944 Education Act included provision for the establishment of institutions called 'County Colleges', to enable young people to continue their education on a part-time or full-time basis after they had left school. Very likely, if we had them, they would be called today 'Colleges of Continuing Education'. The Act, however, made no statutory *requirement* for provision to cater for *all* the various needs, abilities and interests of these young people. So what we got instead were Colleges of *further* Education: institutions which, until recently, have concentrated on vocational and academic needs alone.

So today, further education is the servant of the local labour market, rather than the diverse needs and interests of all young people. It is selective, and its courses are shaped, in the vocational area anyway, by the needs of employers, through the relevant examining bodies. This is similar to the way in which academic courses in schools are shaped by the needs of universities, through

60   *Fit for Work?*

the examining bodies who service them.

Teaching methods in further education tend to be formal. But since only about one third of further education teachers are 'qualified', students do have a greater chance of learning, in the vocational area, at least, both skills and knowledge from the horse's mouth, rather than, as in secondary education, from someone who has read a book about horses. Further education colleges lack the 'pastoral care' interests of the school, and they do not have links with parents, or, very often, with the local community. Sometimes sixteen year olds are considered adults. The colleges are remoter and less accessible than secondary schools, and they do not usually sport the well-organised student bodies found in higher education institutions.

Further education colleges cannot isolate themselves from one important aspect of social and economic life: work, in the day-to-day sense. Many students are only in college part-time, spending the rest of the week in a place of employment for which the education course is helping to fit them. Despite this, the emphasis is on institutional provision, dependent learner-teacher relationships and the focus is on the particular needs of the labour market, which happen to coincide with those of some young people. The difference from school is that the post-sixteen year old can opt out of further education without getting into trouble. This fairly narrow concentration on only a limited part of the wide potential field of continuing education makes these colleges *unsuitable* to a large proportion of young school leavers. Their institutional atmosphere makes them unattractive, particularly to the most alienated school leavers, in spite of the fact that many colleges pride themselves on the way they treat their students as 'grown-ups' rather than children, and many others are proud of their 'responsiveness to local social and community needs and issues'. The meagreness of the grants complete the unattractive picture.

A dangerous attraction

Among young school leavers, there is one group, however, which is very attracted to further education courses. What happens to them may sound a warning to those politicans and professionals who see expanded further education as a way of dealing with rising youth unemployment, now and in the future. This group also has very specific unemployment problems: young Asians.

In a study of Asian school leavers in Walsall in 1975, *(Aspirations*

Versus Opportunities, Dennis Brooks and Karamjit Singh) the
researchers noted in their conclusions:

'In their relative numbers either staying on at school or
continuing their full-time education elsewhere, the Asians are
very different from their white and mostly working class
contemporaries . . . a group far more determined to break out of
the kinds of occupations held by their parents . . . This is not
something self-generated by Asian boys and girls. Rather, it
results from the help, encouragement, and perhaps pressure
from their parents. In part this may be seen as a reaction to race
discrimination: a belief that it is possible to surmount the
discrimination hurdle if formal qualifications are achieved. The
other main element is a desire for upward mobility, and a
willingness and determination to work for it. It is unlikely that
upward mobility is desired for its own sake: rather, it provides the
means for the good life, particularly in material terms.'

This description recalls the pre-war working man's thirst for
education, the aspirations that fed the WEA. A good deal of
professional thinking in further education, adult education and
continuing education still quotes these aspirations as the bedrock of
their belief in education after school. But the foundations look a
little shaky when we see what happens to young people when they
have finished their courses. In a second survey published together
with that carried out in Walsall, a similar group of young Asians
were questioned in Leicester:

'A majority of the Asian sample (55%) was in full-time further
education . . . predominantly on non-vocational courses . . . It is
worth speculating on the fate of this particular section of the
Asian sample, entering the labour market two or three years after
leaving school with (in many cases) only limited additions to their
existing qualifications. For many there is a mistaken belief that
these extra years in the further education sector enhance their
attractiveness to employers. Given the state of the labour market
and the greater selectivity which this allows to employers, it is
probable that these eighteen to nineteen year olds are at a distinct
disadvantage in relation to their younger contemporaries.
Similarly, where age restrictions apply, as in the case of
apprenticeships and occupations requiring defined periods of
training, this can be an inhibiting factor. It is likely that the
expectations raised during the study in the further education

sector will not be met, thus resulting in a group of very frustated teenagers.'

We saw ample evidence that this was so. Transferring the non-vocational offerings of further education colleges to expanded sixth forms, as is planned, will not make the frustration any less. Realism suggests to many young people that this kind of 'more qualification' course will not do them any good as far as job prospects are concerned.

But what it does offer — and this is true of non-vocational courses too — is a chance to push away the moment of decision. There is no need to take the plunge into the *real* world of work for a little longer. Of the young people we talked to, many viewed the further education course they had decided to take with a sense of relief. And many parents also seemed relieved by the prospect:

> 'My Dad says he's not going to let me find a job, it's too big a jump, he says, to go from school to a job. He says he'd rather I stayed on a year, or went to college. And when I had my first interview with the careers teacher, he said the same. They don't want me to work for two or three years. I don't know why: I wanted to get a job myself, but I think it'll be all right at the college — at least it'll be a change from school.'

But when she finishes her course, is this girl going to be faced with exactly the same difficulties that teachers and parents are so happy to see postponed?

The influence of youth unemployment

The influence of growing youth unemployment on further education colleges is by no means confined to the statistical 'buoyancy' we referred to earlier, or to the possibility, growing nearer every day, of considerable expansion not through broadening the scope from *further* to *continuing* in the wider sense, but by the simple expedient of increasing the financial incentives for young people to attend them. Other changes have occurred already, and money is the key to all of them. Just as the lack of money, we presume, originally tailored the idea of County Colleges to the more limited cloth of Further Education, so has the availability of money for particular activities modified the precise nature of the courses many further education colleges offer. These changes have confronted the colleges with one dilemma after another.

For some years, money to run training courses has been available through part of the Manpower Services Commission called the Training Services Division. To get this money the colleges had to satisfy the criteria laid down by the TSD, and many of them were concerned that they were 'no longer masters of our own destiny'. The courses themselves were in the traditional mould of further education, but the participants were not the kind of young people further education had had much to do with. Moreover, they were being paid an allowance that was far larger than the kinds of grants other students were getting! But with money for education, including further education, getting cut back through reductions in public spending, these new resources, available from the MSC, could not be ignored.

From 1975 onwards came new special programmes for the unemployed. The first of these, the Job Creation Programme, wasn't just for young people. It was simply a temporary jobs programme and claimed no concern with education and training needs. But in 1976 the Work Experience Programme arrived, and in order to justify paying participants in this an allowance, rather than a wage (cheaper and easier to administer), it was not just a matter of providing work *experience* rather than work, it was also necessary to have some educational component. Since the sponsors of these schemes were employers of one kind or another, they did not necessarily have any notion of what this educational component should be, or how they could provide it. So these sponsors and the MSC turned for help to local institutions such as colleges of further education.

A new subject was born in further education: 'Life and Social Skills'. Although the MSC claimed to have invented this 'new' subject, it bore a remarkable resemblance to the social education material used in schools. The young people on these work experience courses were even less like the typical further education student than those on the TSD courses. The new courses were originally designed, in a very rough and ready form, by the MSC, although they have since been refined and developed by individuals, authorities and colleges. Sometimes they were offered over a full-time one or two-week period, at other times they were on a half or one day a week 'release' basis.

So the pecking order begins to sort itself out. The best continuing education available to the young person who does not stay in full-time academic or part-time vocational education is a quick two-week dose of sex-education, how-to-present-yourself-at-an-interview, and any other likely looking odds and ends that happen to be around at the time.

But the dilemma is a double one. From the further education point of view it is: do we become involved in different kinds of courses for different kinds of students, just to get hold of the extra resources from the MSC? From the MSC point of view it is: do we encourage the institution-minded further education service to lay on life and social skills and other courses for the participants in special programmes, and force the young people back into those very educational institutions which so many of them have rejected? Both dilemmas became greater in 1978, when the Job Creation Programme came to an end.

In 1978 the £200 million a year Youth Opportunities Programme aimed to provide courses and work experience on a considerably increased scale, and had a target of a quarter of a million young people who might benefit from them. Through this programme a lot of money became available for the 'associated further education' of young people on various types of work experience scheme (though it doesn't actually work out at much per head); there was also a lot of money for training courses. In this situation the dilemmas have become real dangers. The MSC has lacked the will and experience to develop non-institutional education provision, and has and will turn to the colleges. The colleges will continue to refine the 'new' courses for the new clients. And all the people who have a life-time's experience of much more than can be compressed into two weeks of 'life and social skills' won't get a look in.

Whatever happened to the DES?

That question has a simple answer. The Manpower Services Commission was set up, following the 1973 Employment and Training Act, at the very time that cutbacks in public expenditure were making any remaining dreams of improving education and other services — by broader approaches to continuing education, for example — remoter than ever. The fact that employment-related concerns, for better training and manpower planning, had higher political priority than education-related ones, was symbolised by the large amounts of money poured by government ministers into the MSC's coffers. The Department of Education and Science (DES) looked on powerless and, it seemed, pretty witless too. The army of Her Majesty's Inspectorate, labouring round the country with briefcases pregnant with good practice, did not seem to notice that more and more young people were leaving school less and less equipped to deal with the world that awaited them, nor that more and more of them were becoming unemployed. Then, when inflation became an even higher political priority than unemployment, the educational issues and possibilities slipped to an even lower place in the ratings. All the education officials could do, it seemed, was snap in irritated fashion at the heels of the MSC.

Perhaps that is unfair, because besides money, power and wit, the MSC had an important extra advantage over the DES. This was the ability to deliver services *directly,* through means which it could devise itself. As we shall describe, it chose the delivery route of sponsorship: saying to colleges, employers and many others, 'If you will do this, we will give you the money'. The DES, as any Secretary of State knows, has to get local education authorities to do and deliver. That takes a long time — look at the establishment of comprehensive education!

The department does have some modest achievements to boast about — although these have been viewed with glee or disdain in various quarters. There is Unified Vocational Preparation, for example. This is a scheme, jointly financed by MSC and the DES, to develop 'new kinds of vocational preparation attractive to the young employee and employer alike'. It is for the young *employed,* then, albeit for those, 'usually on the lower CSE levels', that is, those young people who are less likely to benefit from in-company or in-college training and education programmes. UVP is run along the MSC's favoured sponsorship lines, the schemes can be based in college, in company, in both, or even in youth centres. The DES information says: 'The objectives of UVP is (sic) to provide a vocationally-orientated development prgramme which will . . . improve the individual's self-confidence, motivation and commitment to work by . . .'

This looks like a bit of the old 'Life and Social Skills,' and various other odds and ends which place it, as far as educational quality is concerned, above what the unemployed get and below what the college-goers get. Another level in the pecking other, then.

Even three years after the establishment of the first of the MSC's special programmes for the unemployed, the DES continued to do little or nothing. Perhaps that is a good thing. The new developments it proposes are educational maintenance awards to encourage more young people to enter full-time further education, and the establishment of a DES controlled committee to look at the 16-19 'problem' which issued a 'discussion paper' in February 1979 which was thin and uninspiring. In addition, the Department has established a Further Education Curriculum Review and Development Unit, which has carried out a postal survey.

The activities of the Department of Education in Northern Ireland provide an interesting contrast. There is much more vigour and imagination there, developing new ideas (like courses which are not based in colleges of further education), and, more important, developing new ways to implement them.

A familiar story

What is happening now, and likely to happen in the future, is a classic example of the way existing institutions take over a new need and problem and fit it to their policy — the institutionally determined response. These institutions, like schools, close down for long periods every year, on the assumption that the problems they deal with follow the same cycles as medieval agriculture.

Once again, responses where individual and collective action are paramount will be found only at the fringes, though a certain amount of 'conscience money' has gone from the MSC (not the DES!) to such alternatives. An example is the 'Just the Job' scheme, invented by the National Extension College, a pioneering voluntary organisation active in the continuing education field. This uses TV programmes, lively 'kits' and volunteer workers, to help young unemployed people, working individually and collectively, to do something about their predicament. Of course, television producers, like the principals of further education colleges, guard their right to determine what is the right material for the young unemployed person. Even where there is money around, good ideas won't always flourish.

The one lobby organisation which seemed to be representing the interests of the young unemployed was Youthaid. When it was established and began campaigning on behalf of the young and unemployed, early in 1977, it was a militant and quite useful organisation. It had some rows with the MSC and flourished on leaked documents, clandestine meetings with well-placed officials and all the cloak-and-dagger stuff of campaign, pressure and lobby. But it grew research-biased, getting grants from the EEC and OECD to carry out surveys of school leavers and the like. Then it successfully bid for a 'research' contract from the Further Education Curriculum Review and Development Unit at the DES, to work on 'further education curriculum alternatives for areas of high and prolonged youth unemployment'. 'Curriculum alternatives' does not look too encouraging, and the project, like the DES Unit, does not apply to *continuing* education, but *further* education. Youthaid have been quieter in their championship of the young unemployed since they received grants from both the DES and the MSC. So the *pressure* for alternatives grows weaker.

Informal education

The more informal kinds of continuing education, as delivered to post-sixteen year olds by the education services, are collectively described as 'youth and community' or 'community education' services. *Adult* education comes under this heading, and further education, too, in those local authorities eager to demonstrate their commitment to 'womb to tomb' education. The outward and visible sign of this philosophy is the large, all-purpose institution, offering everything from secondary school to sauna bath. Henry Morris originally imagined the development of centres like village shops and pubs, where this cradle-to-grave education would be available. Instead the tendency has been to produce hypermarkets of community activity, with the goods pre-wrapped for those able to get to them. Young people do not find these places immediately congenial, and they tend to appeal to an older age group. Sometimes these hypermarkets have further education colleges hidden away inside them.

Youth and community education services are the poor relations of the rest of the education service. Local authorities are not obliged to provide many of them, and they are not only poorly resourced, but easy targets for cuts in public expenditure. Less than one per cent of recurrent expenditure in education goes on youth work, and for those purposes a youth is defined as someone over 14. Activities for and with young people below that age have to be self-financing. A good deal of the 'less than one per cent' goes to provision-oriented services. A very tiny fraction goes to those organisations which try to give young people a role in which they are *not clients*. We have already said that the organisations which provide for young people are quick to make sure that they control what happens to new sources of funding like the Silver Jubilee Trust, so that these cannot be used for new practices. The DES hands out very small amounts of money to national voluntary organisations, but though these are non-statutory in name, in fact, their practice is to *provide for* young people. The even smaller amount of money which the DES has ear-marked for innovative experimental projects is channelled through an organisation called the National Council for Voluntary Youth Services, which has little contact with young people themselves, and no ability to encourage experiment. The Youth Service Forum, also set up by the DES, enables representatives of various important youth organisations to talk . . . they seem to find things to talk about. No Minister, senior or junior, in any recent government, has taken a positive and vigorous lead in the youth field, and the result is that civil servants from the DES do nothing but form alliances with dull and unimaginative 'youth' organisations. That is the state of youth work.

In the round of regional conferences that launched the Great Debate about education, young people were conspicuously thin on the ground, and youth organisations weren't represented. The one government department which does make money available for non-paternalist youth work is the Voluntary Services Unit at the Home Office. But grants from this department are subject to the scrutiny of the civil servants from the DES. The comment from one official there, on an application for funds for a multi-racial project aiming to produce non-racialist books for young people, was: 'I am not sure I would want my daughter to read one of these books.' When one of us presented a paper to the Manpower Services Commission about the possibility, which became a reality, of a community service element in the new special programmes for young unemployed people, the comment from the DES was: Why not operate this element of the programme through a national youth organisation rather than through local initiative? The organisation suggested was one that had given up its 'youth' orientation some years previously.

We give these anecdotal references to suggest that the ignorance and lack of imagination of the 'leadership' coming from the government department responsible, is encouraging youth work to be paternalist and dedicated to maintaining the 'client' role of the young. This is the same department that is responsible for the dull narrow-mindedness of further education.

The odd guru and odder politician does, sometimes, see lessons in those situations where the young are given *roles*. They quote places like Cuba, where young people cut cane, or Belfast, where they chuck rocks. It is not impossible to see a purpose to youth, and to realise that fencing young people in, whether in football grounds or youth clubs, is compounding the youth problem, not easing it.

One energetic and young MP introduced, as a private member, a 'Youth and Community' Bill, some years ago. This was imaginative in its vision of young people participating in local affairs and local decision-making processes. But the government of the day talked it out, and the MP lost his seat at the next general election.

Is it naive to talk of leadership in this field? Of course, the DES cannot tell local authorities how to spend the money they get from the rates and from central government through the rate support grant. But it is possible to lead through force of ideas as well as force of discipline.

8 Community Education

In the youth services the crisis is as much one of direction as of resources. The hopeful aspect is the fact that the great majority of youth workers are not full-time employees of the youth service, they are people who have other jobs during the day, but who work in youth clubs in the evening. They are either paid on a sessional basis — a few pounds per night — or they are volunteers. A lecturer in youth work estimated four years ago that there were only approximately 3000 full-time posts in the service, compared with 250,000 part-timers and volunteers. (Michael Woolley, TES June 1975) The figures are probably not much changed. So this service has a very solid lay base. A lot of ordinary people are involved in it.

Although much of youth work means getting young people into youth clubs or youth organisations, although there is this 'institution' mentality, the style of youth work is often *informal*. This contrasts with the style of school and further education. Of course, the directive approach can be very formal; and informality brings its own problems. Young people, schooled to associate institutions with formality, may vary in their reaction from stupefied aimlessness to uncontrollable testing of the adult workers, who become patrolling policemen.

Many young people prefer commercially organised activities, or their own, do-it-yourself activities, or no activities at all, to the offerings of the youth service. This speaker is about to leave school:

'I've never liked youth clubs, never. I used to go to one and there used to be vicars and that there, and you can't eat chewing gum and "You must put the plastic cups in the box at the end". Me brother runs a disco and I go out with him. It's for under-eighteens — we go there to about ten, then we go to the pub.'

There are other distinctions in youth services. There are statutory youth services, which are paid for and organised by the employees of local authorities, and there are voluntary youth services, run by organisations with an independent, often charitable status. These range from the Scout Associations and the National Association of Youth Clubs, to small clubs run by local churches. The word voluntary does not mean that the services are wholly run by volunteers. It means *non-statutory*. And the word voluntary does not mean that what is on offer is much different from what is on offer in the local authority youth clubs, because the aim is still that of provision for youth.

We are trying to emphasise that there is little *alternative* youth work just as there is little *alternative* education. There is no money for it. The voluntary organisations are happy to deliver services for the statutory authorities, and that is what they get central and local government grants for. The total *range* of what is available, just as in secondary education, just as in further education, is sadly limited. What is on offer suits some young people, some of the time. The rest vote with their feet.

The arrival of the Manpower Services Commission on this scene, with its hundreds of millions of pounds to spend on the young unemployed, provoked varied responses among those dealing with young people through 'youth work'.

The youth service response to unemployment

Response number one didn't actually need MSC money and pre-dated its availability in many places. MSC money helped with paying the necessary extra staff. This response was to open youth clubs and centres during the day, for recreational activities. We might call this 'Return and yawn', though many young people were grateful for the chance to get in out of the cold, to get away from home. The motivation was to get them off the streets and keep them out of trouble. The next speaker manages a centre for the young unemployed which has social facilities alongside special training courses. These social facilities have been open in the evenings, but it is proving impossible to continue with this arrangement:

'Last winter we would have six people in and they would all be drop-outs. We were providing warmth and cheap drink and a base for whipping out and whipping somebody's handbag. I simply hadn't realised that there were so many young people, sixteen, seventeen year olds, who are literally walking the country. The news got round that we were open and were a good touch. Soon the message got round that this was the place where the deviant fringe came — so nobody else did come. And it dawned on us that the people we had coming in were what the youth service calls the "unclubbables". The youth service clearly don't have a clue what to do with "unclubbables", and they haven't given us one piece of concrete advice as to what we should do with these people. That's why we close our social centre in the evenings.'

The second response was to say that unemployed young people were the business of the Careers Service and the MSC and nothing to do with youth workers. Sometimes this response derived from experiences like that just described.

Thirdly, many statutory and voluntary youth services saw a chance to do something about that 3000:250,000 professional:lay ratio in the youth service. Why not use the government funds, available from 1975 onwards, through the original Job Creation Programme, to recruit extra staff? After all, the aim of the programme was to make work of 'social and community benefit'. The initial difficulties were recurrent. The Job Creation Programme was designed to fund schemes providing short-term work, usually through construction, destruction, renovation and conservation projects. Once you've planted the trees, levelled the slag heap, drained the marsh, the job is done. But there was nothing 'temporary' about working as an assistant, government-funded youth worker. The maximum length of stay in these government schemes, Job Creation Programme or Youth Opportunities Programme, is one year. So turnover became inevitable in a field of work where continuity is quite important, and the government funds strengthened the paternalist, professional, institution-minded approach.

The same talk goes on in the youth service as in the other public services about the 'profession': about qualifications, rules of entry and training. A year's experience as an assistant youth worker is not enough to qualify the person who has it for entry to the youth work profession. All it might do is provide that person with the motivation for a type of work which he or she can only enter if they are prepared to spend some time in the appropriate training courses. So many of these schemes provided for the older and better-qualified unemployed — recent graduates, for example.

The fourth response is rather exciting, and it is the very opposite to the second response. It only began with the introduction of the Youth Opportunities Programme in 1978, because this programme was exclusively directed at the *young* unemployed. Among the earlier programmes, prior to 1978, the Work Experience

Programme, established in 1976 and taken into the YOP as one part of it in 1978, was for the benefit of young people only but was aimed at private employers; while the Job Creation Programme was not meant for young people alone.

This response said: Why can't the youth and community services act as sponsors of any or all of the wide range of training and work experience opportunities for young people? Particularly since the aim of the programme seems to be non-institution-based education, work experience-based education, rather: learning on the spot, at first hand, from the horse's mouth — experiential learning. Of course, not everybody leapt at this as an idea, and of course part of the reason for this response from the youth and community service was money. The starving service saw and responded to what one youth service administrator called 'a Klondike'. But others put it another way as 'a chance to do realistic and relevant things with and for the group of young people who had had little to do with us and who we had never been able to reach out to in the past.'

It wasn't just local authorities, but voluntary organisations, too, who decided to strike it rich with this response. It offered, quite simply, a way to put 'informal social education' into a more realistic context than sitting around in a coffee bar in the youth centre: into an 'experience' context.

This response has not been widespread. The earliest example of it is the 'Old Fire Station' in Coventry, and this owed its establishment more to the work of further education people and a vigorous-minded local authority administration, than to youth service workers. It also owed its development to the simple fact that the local authority was prepared to put money into the Old Fire Station, a social and training centre, and also into the establishment of a compact and determined team, at a high level in the administration, to take concerted action on youth unemployment.

More recently Strathclyde and Essex have begun to develop their own youth and community responses to the Youth Opportunities Programme. In both authorities this has come about because of a combination of imagination and opportunism in the senior officials concerned, and a willingness to invest and re-direct resources in the direction of youth unemployment. Strathclyde has appointed large numbers of extra staff, with its own money, to help with the administration as well as the educational aspects of the new schemes for young unemployed people. Essex has developed an imaginative approach to the work by basing new, 'all-purpose youth opportunity centres' on its existing youth and community centres, so that young people can find the kind of opportunity which bests suits them by simply coming through one door, rather than being sent from one separately organised scheme to another. Both these authorities have tried hard to appoint non-professional, 'unqualified' but highly *experienced* people, though it has not been easy, for existing professional associations and unions don't like it.

This seems a good approach, and may be one of the most important results of the intervention of the Manpower Services Commission. But it is important to ask if we are seeing the foundation of a new bureaucratic empire? Isn't there a danger that this response will become as remote and provision-oriented as the rest of the youth/education system? Will this response also exclude the possibility of individual and collective responses to this problem?

Adult education

This is available to everyone, even before they have left school. The offerings are a mixture of academic courses, so that those who failed at school have another chance, at 'night school', and of non-vocational, cultural classes. The trouble is, the students have to pay for it. These fees don't cover all the costs, but this is an area of education where *net* expenditure by authorities is minute. There is no defined statutory obligation on local authorities to provide adult education, the only pressure is that of demand from potential students and from particular social needs, like adult illiteracy.

Those public expenditure cuts, which began soon after local government reorganisation in 1974, hit adult education hard. Provision was reduced and fees went up. The result was that any inroads adult education had made into attracting non-middle class participants disappeared quickly, leaving a middle-class mainstream plus those from variously defined 'social need' groups, who did not have to pay, or who paid a reduced rate.

So there are, in reality, two quite distinct adult education services. The first is basically a commercial undertaking, purveying what those of us who can afford it want, and carefully switching 'profits' from the most popular items to the less profitable. The second is essentially a 'remedial' service for those 'in distress' categories, financed by external funds. Adult illiterates are the best known category here. Lacking is a middle-ground between these two. We have often heard people say that adult education should 'help people cope with change and master it'. But there is a growing inability among most people to cope with, involve themselves in, change and master the many institutions by which they are dominated. You cannot simply educate people into roles, so that they develop the ability they need, but education is a *part* of the process. Any programme for action, whether concerned with the needs and aspirations of the unemployed or of those rendered helpless by the institutional tendencies of a modern state, must recognise the need for continuing education to be available, and for it to have a style and basis for entry which does not simply narrow its focus to those who can buy it or to those deemed in need of 'provision'.

It seems absurd that with unemployment high and likely to remain high for some time, not just among young people, adult and continuing education still labours, making do on insufficient money. It is easy to criticise it for its style, institutional mentality, its faithful following of the school term cycle — also characteristic of the youth service — which means that it closes down at weekends and in the holidays: the very time when many people can devote themselves to other pursuits than paid work.

The adult literacy 'remedial' programme is an interesting illustration of the possibilities for doing things differently, and it has lessons for those trying to counter the new and developing state of unemployment. This programme didn't group people together in classes and institutions to teach them to read and write. It recognised two things: that such an approach would merely repeat the very circumstances which had caused the problem in the first place; and that many perfectly ordinary people can read and write and, with a modicum of help, can acquire the confidence and skills needed to work with the illiterate on a one-to-one basis. So first of all the programme rejected the obvious 'more of the same' approach.

Then it ignored the common warning against trying to work with lay, or non-professional, people. This claims that such efforts will fail because they are idealistic, people are too interested in their own concerns, don't want to help others, expect the institutions of the state, for which they pay, to solve these problems for them. The astounding success of the adult literacy movement seems to show the opposite. In three years, 80,000 voluntary, unpaid tutors were recruited, and they provided tuition for 125,000 adults. If you ask those tutors about their work, they frequently say that they don't see themselves as *helping*, they are meeting their own need to be involved in problems which are public, not professional, property. The operation has become known as a 'movement', rather than the more institutional-sounding 'programme'. Although the success of this movement looks rather more limited when viewed against the background of 2 million illiterates in Britain it does show that imagination and initiative can make things happen. It was the energetic work of the British Association of Settlements which led to central government establishing and funding the Adult Literacy Resource Agency, and the BBC carried on the momentum:

> 'Some local authorities would not have provided the support they had over the past three years unless the BBC had taken the initiative . . . The BBC broadcasts — On the Move and Your Move — had forced local authorities to respond.' *(Guardian,* September 1978)

Now the movement is entirely in the hands of local authorities. One can only hope it doesn't proceed to roll down the institutional hill, as the stick and carrot function of the Adult Literacy Resource Agency disappears. It seems foolish to dispense with this agency, for many other central 'resourcing' institutions could learn from its work. The Voluntary Services Unit in the Home Office, for example, has done little to use its funds (over £2 million) as a stick or carrot to encourage the development of alternative approaches to other sectors of public services.

9 Fewer Jobs — Plenty of Advice

We must now look at other people and other services which, together with those in the previous chapters, complete the picture of what is available to the young school leaver. Some of these, like the Careers Service and the Manpower Services Commission, are directly involved in helping young people to find and equip themselves for work. Others, like parents, friends and neighbours, do not seem to be directly involved but are, we have found, extremely important.

The professional advice system

To begin with, there is the Careers Service. Unlike the directly 'interventionist' MSC programmes, this service is operated by education authorities. But it exists alongside another statutory service which helps people locate jobs and vice versa. This is the employment service operated by the MSC. And then there are the private employment agencies and services, which range from advertisements in newsagents' windows to Brook Street Bureau and Alfred Marks. The statutory employment services have responded to the challenge of private enterprise by moving out of their dowdy, back-street employment offices into prime-site high street premises, complete with carpet tiles and modern furniture. Job Centres have arrived. And, of course, some young people use these services. And more and more of them do so as they progress from 16 to 17 to 18 to 19 and realise that they are not kids any longer. The services offered are more adult in style: display boards and self-service.

The Careers Service is like many other public services, personal in style, not inclined towards the self-reliant, self-initiated approach of the Job Centre. It is oriented to provision, with the young person as client, someone who needs help and protection. The name 'Careers Service' is a bad mistake. We have already seen that many young people, contemplating the move from school, consider a 'career' to be something for the favoured and qualified few, something associated with qualifications, promotion patterns, yearly increments. Of those we asked, few considered their parents to be in a 'career'. When we questioned what they thought a career was, the answers they gave were 'being a teacher' and 'being a doctor'.

'Careers Guidance', as it is called, begins earlier than the date of leaving school, through careers teachers, who are a sort of outpost of the local authority's careers guidance and advice system. This system is based on Careers Officers, who begin their contact with young people around the time of school leaving. But by the time this meeting occurs, some young people have already decided that, on the evidence of the 'careers' advice they've already had from careers teachers, little good will come of it. Others have a different, equally unrealistic expectation: that the Careers Officer *will get them a job*.

We want to stress how important names are in this game. Careers guidance is a bad name, and it leads to confusion among young people. To say what you want to be during your careers lessons and interviews, you have to find a *name* for it. So, in one low stream class in the third year at a comprehensive school, all the girls we spoke to knew what they wanted to do: 'be a nurse' or 'work with children'. We thought this ambition derived most of all from the familiarity of the name, a common name, one they knew, one which they knew that we knew. It's *careers* that have names, and it seems possible that it is this 'can you name it?' question which causes worries about evidently high and unrealistic expectations among young people at school. Our impression was that these girls neither expected nor wanted to be nurses. They just knew the name.

As young people get older, through friends, through relatives and through their own developing understanding and contact, they come to realise and be realistic about their own life and job-chances. The pendulum often seems to swing the other way. An attitude of resigned helplessness and hopelessness sets in among the low achievers. Expectations become mere dreams, and an acceptance of low station and dismal prospect appears. In some areas there is also an acceptance of likely unemployment for at least some periods of time. There is a real period of transition, beginning as late as the last year at school, from unrealistically high aspirations to unrealistically low ones. For those who cannot find work, this transition leads to depression, frustration and, eventually, total loss of confidence.

Then comes the contact with Careers Officers. These officers are closer to the real job market than any other official they've met. Careers Officers get vacancies from employers — though we shouldn't forget that 'young people only' jobs are getting fewer and fewer.

This fact in itself seems to argue against a 'young persons' employment service', which would seem a more accurate description of what young people with these expectations need. There is the belief among some young people that to get a job you need only to go 'down the Careers'. The Careers Officer is a kind of dope-peddler — you can only get it from him. This shows how clearly ill-prepared these particular young people are for the work aspect of the outside world. It is, admittedly, a positive and hopeful view of the Careers Service that they are starting out with. But, for young people used to the dependent, caring-professional world of school, the Careers Service is bound to look and feel familiar.

The realisation dawns that the Careers Office is not a magic open-sesame to work and the emerging adult, forced out of the chrysalis by this post-school period of rude awakening, finds that he is once more a victim, at the mercy of yet another professional service. Here is a report of a discussion with a group of young men. There are four of them;

Has anyone been up there [the Careers Office]?
A: I been going there for ages . . .
B: I got a job from there . . . yeah . . . a furniture shop . . . eighteen quid a week . . .

What happens when you go up the careers then?
B: I'll tell you from me experience. First of all he sent me a letter one day . . . and he said he would like to see me.
C: Because he 'adn't been for two weeks . . .
B: . . . so I went up and saw 'im, and he sits there looking and tappin' 'is pen . . .
C: . . . get on with it then . . .
B: . . . and says . . .
D: Speak up a bit lad!
B: From what I see of your record you're interested in . . . Yes, that's right.
D: Well, we've got nowt. (Laughter)
B: . . . Well, we've got nothing in at the moment, but when there is, we'll keep in touch . . . Is there nothing else you'd be interested in? . . . ah well, I have a few cards here . . . and he rings up and says 'Ere we are, we've got an

appointment . . . go gown and see this bloke tomorrow . . .
(David Sawdon and Robert Adams, *Actions*, January 1979)

So that's what it is like. Keep in touch, we care about you. We can't help you with what you want, but hold on while we try something else for you. It is noticeable that the young person doesn't define his needs, the Careers Officer does that for him.

Careers advice is also offered by the service. This is useful to some young people, confusing to others, who can't see if it's the key to job-getting or not. Besides, for many life has been so full of friendly professional 'advice' that the thought of more is intolerable. Nothing the others said was any use, why should this person be different? Some young people are afraid that their 'record' allows the adviser to pass on information to employers before they even get a look at you. Your 'record' includes things like your truancy from school, your lack of qualifications, the colour of your skin. The Careers Service are keen on "confidentiality" — a favourite professional word — to the point of refusing to give names and addresses of young people to interview for a book like this. But many young people suspect that the access of the Careers Officer to the ear of the prospective employer will prejudice their chances. They may be wrong, but that's what they fear.

How young people regard the Careers Service

So the service offers help, advice and job-finding, and the offerings are successful for *some* young people. For others the Careers Service has little help and is sometimes an obstruction. These are those same bottom-of-the-pile young people we keep coming back to. The rub is that vacancies are notified to the service, by employers who expect to be sent the right raw material, and as we have said, it is these employers who must face the morality of their selective attitudes. But other problems can be laid at the door of the service itself. It perpetuates 'dependence on institutions' and 'second-hand advice', two familiar and unsuitable experiences for many young people. It is a system geared to the more able and the demands of the labour market. It tries to pretend that it is suitable for the less fortunate young person, and that it is a 'caring' service. Perpetuation of childhood again, as the Careers Officer leafs through the vacancy information book and arranges an interview on behalf of the 'client'. It is necessary to have a personal service to offer to a young person, lost in the post-school world. At the opposite extreme the self-service system of the Job-Centre can be heart-breaking. But to confine this service to a single, second-hand institution, that is insensitive. Here is a girl talking about her first visit to the Careers Office, in her last term at school:

'The Careers Officer asked me what I wanted to be and I told her school was getting a real drag, and she kept on saying "You can stay on in the sixth form." And I'd already said I was getting fed up of school. I wanted her to help me with what to do, and she didn't at all, she confused me. Waste of time, it was. I was with her about fifteen minutes, but I don't think she wanted to know anything about me. I felt rather un-comfortable because what I told, she took it the opposite. She kept on saying "Sixth form would be the best idea for you". But when I'd talked things over with the careers teacher at school, I'd come out all confident, you know . . .'

Here are other comments on experiences at the Careers Office:

'You have to go down there every day before they send you for an interview — they have favourites down there.'

One boy, out of work for six months since he left school, saw the Careers Office as an extension of the familiar education system:

'At school, they gave us a few lessons on leaving. 'What are you going to be?" And then you tell 'em and they, like, forget about it. They probably pass it on to the Careers Centre about a week before you leave. When I went down to the Careers Centre this woman just asked me what kind of job I wanted, would I accept another job when it came up. All these questions. They're not very interested, but they ask 'em.'

The next girl felt that the Careers Service was a real danger to her:

'I'm afraid of the Careers Officers. They're helpful in some ways, but not when they're trying to push you into doing things. I'm not very confident and I easily get pushed into doing things.'

It's probably as well that schools do not consider the development of initiative and self-confidence as a high priority, because the lack of those qualities in the school leavers who come to them suits the Careers Service very well. As far as we can see Careers Officers do not strive to encourage the development of these qualities but rather, as with other sectors of education we have described, aim to make the 'client' fit the service, not vice versa. Again, this works for some of the clients, some of the time. But it fails an awful lot of them.

How do young people look for jobs? Their use of the services varies according to age. Those under 17 are more likely to be still 'with' the Careers Service; those over 17 are more likely to use the Employment Office or Job Centre. The MSC survey of unemployed 16-18-year-olds recorded these answers to questions about *where* young people looked for jobs (at the time of the survey):

Newspapers	64%
Careers Office	40%
Employment Office/Job Centre	54%
Direct approach to employers	52%
Ask friends/acquaintances	22%
Ask parents/relatives	17%
Private employment agency	2%
Other	1%
Doing nothing	7%

That suggests that the Careers Service is not considered useful by more than half of the unemployed school leavers. The survey also noted these as 'typical comments' from young people on why they went to the Careers Office less frequently as time when on:

'Because there is nothing there. Every time you go, there are loads of you all being sent after one job. You never get a job from them.'

'They were not helpful . . . they had no jobs left by the time I got there. Mind you, I suppose it's my own fault. I never used to get there until 12 o'clock and all the jobs had gone, except for those with 'O' levels and that.'

'They try to help you but they can't get jobs out of thin air for you.'

'You get to saying to yourself what's the point in going.'

'They didn't seem to help me at all. After about a month I stopped going. They never even looked for jobs, didn't tell me I could register for work at the Job Centre.'

There are no such typical comments listed for the adult employment services, though the survey does acknowledge that these are impersonal. There is a contrast between the loving care of the Careers Service, however ineffectual this may prove, and the take-it-or-leave-it style of the Employment Services. In the same survey it was recorded that 30% of those young people using the Careers Service, when asked about the help and advice given, said 'Gave no specific help or advice'. 43% of those using Job or Employment Centres answered in the same way.

This is a specific example of the 'more of the same' approach of a public service institution. Each year the Careers Service is strengthened. More money is found for new posts, and these are often called 'unemployment specialists'. But all the evidence and comment points to the failure of the Careers Service to make any real impact on the predicament of the young unemployed. So is it really sensible to appoint more officers? Wouldn't it be more sensible to investigate alternative ways of supporting young job seekers?

Genuine alternatives, like the National Extension College's 'Just the Job', are starved of financial support, and the Institute of Careers Officers trots out the well-worn argument, 'if we had more staff, we'd do a better job'. Since 1975 the Careers Service has been strengthened by over 320 posts. That costs £1.5 millions annually. Some of these posts are for special 'outreach' careers officers, to try to work with those young people who reject the whole system. And the Institute of Careers Officers wants these workers based in the Careers Office. It seems that the need for some radical and different approach is realised. But is it realised *why* the approach must be different, and why the present system is unacceptable to so many young people?

The next comment, from a girl, points to the gulf that exists between individual action — through newspaper advertisements, in this case — and institutional action, through the Careers Service. It is this gulf that needs filling with approaches like 'Just the Job', with its network of volunteer counsellors and friendly adults:

> 'I get very, very nervous about interviews. I've got one tomorrow and I'm very frightened. I'll have to go out tonight and calm myself. It's for a receptionist job in John _____'s. I saw the advert in the paper, so I just rang up and made the appointment. I did it myself, nothing to do with the Careers Office. They don't seem to do anything for you, they just say, "Wait, wait, we'll let you know".'

Just as there are greater levels of 'faith' in the education system among young Asians, so surveys among young Asians and young West Indians (*Aspirations versus Opportunities; Looking for Work, a Survey of Black school leavers in Lewisham,* Community Relations Commission), reveal a greater dependence among all of them on the Careers Service, than among a comparable sample of young whites. As one might expect, more young blacks get their jobs via that route than do young whites. The Walsall/Leicester study said:

'. . . Asians, as immigrants or children of immigrants, would not have access to so many informal networks to potential employers. Second, parents or other relatives who are often important in recommending and placing white working class school leavers would not, in the Asian case, be so well placed to influence personnel managers or other employers' representatives. Race is relevant here, and it is important to the third consideration: Asians are rejected for racial reasons; the official agencies to some extent are able to circumvent racial discrimination. For these reasons, therefore, the Asians are very much more dependent on the official agencies. The whites, by contrast, have easier access to informal networks, they can be 'spoken for' by parents, other relatives or friends, and they can apply personally with a greater prospect of success.'

The Lewisham survey seems to convey similar conclusions about young West Indians, though for them, the result is often to drop out, into an out-of-contact sub-culture which youth workers call 'unattached' and the Careers Service call 'unregistered'. This subculture survives on petty crime rather than state benefit. For young blacks who are more reliant on the system, it is inevitable that there should be a greater sense of alienation from the system when it fails them.

Other sources of advice and support

If we recognise that young people get help and advice from other sources than the official services, whether these be the media, parents, friends or anyone else, then it seems time to consider how these other sources can be improved and developed. For they are supplementing the institutional service with individual and collective action, and some young people are finding that this supplement best suits their needs.

It is also becoming apparent that we cannot divorce 'work' or

'careers' help and advice from actual experiences of work and
from help and advice which is aimed at alternatives to work and
employment. It seems a waste of energy for a young person, or
any person, to have to trek from a youth counsellor or a Citizens'
Advice Bureau to a youth worker,   careers officer, employment
officer, employer, probation officer, social worker, community
worker and so on, as each of them deal with different 'bits' of the
problem. And it is not enough for these people to meet and talk
about you at one of their once-a-month lunches or case
conferences. Because you are not simply a 'case' and because you
are involved with other people: friends and parents, acquaintances
and relatives.

The part these other people play in education and work-choice
cannot be assessed statistically, and we have relied for our information about their role on the conversations we have had with
young people. Friends tend to be almost exactly your own age,
when you are young. This is because schools organise young
people into 'years' and the school day means that young people
in any one year tend to spend their time together. We were told
that within school it was essential to be part of a group of
friends, since this group provided a defence against other groups
of young people:

'If you don't have mates other kids gang up on you.'

We asked if these friendships would continue when the young
people had left school. Many assumed that they would not:

'You don't have friendships like that when you leave school,
not unless you go on the dole. You're always bound to meet
somebody in the dole queue that you know. You go along and
sign on the same day as someone else and get to know them.'

Although that speaker was still at school himself, he had several
brothers who had left school, and his comments drew on their
experience.

Within school your 'mates' can have an influence on the actual
subjects you choose to study:

'We all put the same lessons as our friends down when it comes
to choosing subjects. It's just as well me and my friend both
want a job that needs the same subjects. One girl in my class
chose the hardest subjects on the list — computer studies,
extra maths — just because her friend chose them and was the
only one doing them. But she hasn't got the brains for it, she's

just doing it to be with her friend.'

But there was also a recognition that close friendships can interfere with the way that you study your subjects:

'Some people find it easier to work on their own, rather than
with friends who talk all the time. But if I've got no friends I
really feel miserable, it really depresses me.'

For many young people these friendships will not survive school-
leaving, especially if the school draws young people from a wide
area. They may simply live too far away from you. This is
another shock for the sixteen-year-old leaver. The world is no
longer full of people of the same age. It never was, but school
fostered the illusion. Further education offers a chance to prolong
companionship with your peers. Often work does not.

Among young women it seems that friends can influence your
work-choice in the same way as they influence your subject choice.
Many girls were applying together for jobs in the same company,
or training courses in the same college. We were impressed that
this need to do things together was stronger in young women than
young men. On the other hand, we saw examples of friendships
among young men that had survived school-leaving, but these
tended to be rooted in some out-of-school interest. Two seventeen
year olds work in different businesses on opposite sides of a large
town, but they see one another nearly every evening to work on
an old motor-car. The friendship extends to the older brothers in
each family, and in both cases these brothers had helped the two
young men to find their jobs.

It was interesting to see how often this happened. Very many
young school-leavers have friendships with slightly older young
people, usually in the 19-25 age group. These friendships do not
begin at school. A common feature of them was an element of
admiration for the older person and a gratitude for the 'adult'
way in which they were treated by him or her. The next
girl, for example, told us about a young married woman
neighbour:

'I met her when I was in fourth year. I was walking down the
street and I heard someone shout to me and it was Pauline. I
knew her to talk to, but not as a proper friend. She says, "Are you
coming round later, because I'm by meself?" She was expecting
then. So I says, "All right then, I'll come and keep you
company." And I went down there and I've been going down

there ever since. I baby-sit for her once a week and if I'm baby-sitting next-door I take her baby in there with me. The baby's lovely but she's got something wrong with her. We're taking her down to London next month to see a specialist.'

This girl takes her problems and worries to her older friend and has discussed her future with her. It is clear that the friend also shares her problems.

It was often this question — 'Where do you go if something is worrying you?' — which revealed the existence of these friendships with slightly older people. Sometimes these people were simply brothers and sisters, more frequently they were the friends of older brothers and sisters. It goes without saying that they are people with experience of job-getting and, sometimes, unemployment. They know what it is like to be confused, but they have usually managed to cope themselves. With the admiration for them, there goes a desire to 'be like them' — to imitate. Imitation is a form of learning for which schools are not well-equipped. Having 'coped', with their own situation, these friends sometimes 'fix' things up for young school-leavers. This girl has an older boy-friend who has done exactly that for her brother:

'I was talking to me boy-friend about me brother being out of work. He says, "I might be able to get him a job." So I told him what he could do, and my boy-friend put his name in at the place where he worked, and my brother got an interview and got the job. I think my boy-friend just had a word with one of the gaffers, saying he knew a person who needed a job, and the gaffer took it from there. I think the job's something to do with cutting metal. If you've got a couple of friends who can put a good word in for you, you stand a better chance of getting a job.'

This kind of story was repeated often by unemployed school leavers. The jobs obtained in this way did not seem to be intrinsically more desirable than a job you might get via the Careers Office. But the means of obtaining them was considered more acceptable. One boy had got a job lined up 'with one of me brother's mates'. His friend had got a job with another contact of the same brother. Older friends were also a source of practical information:

'How did you know about signing on the dole?
My Dad didn't know, only my friend did. And my Mum has some friends and she knows what their sons are doing. My friend Ayub is older than me and he tells me what to do. I see him

nearly every night. Sometimes we watch television, sometimes I help him make amplifiers or something he's building. We've talked about opening a business together, me and him. Because he could teach me servicing. The majority of the time he does his friends' servicing and sometimes he shows me what's wrong with them. Usually he gives me a television and tells me to find out what's wrong with it, and if I can't, then he shows me. He's doing a three year course at the moment and he'll end up with HNC. He's good, he knows all about the stuff I don't know, and he has all the meters and things, and he teaches me about them.'

That young man had only been in employment for four months since he left school two years before. So his admiration for the skills and confidence of his friend is supplemented by the learner/teacher relationship he describes. Another boy had formed similar relationships with older men who had taught him about pigeon-fancying — a hobby he took up when his father died. These 'older friends' have not necessarily been successful at school. In fact, they often seem to have done badly, but they have generally found work and are doing well at it:

'When he first left school, he told me, the only thing he wanted to do was to be a furniture remover and drive a furniture van. He did it for about six months and then this bloke said to him: "Why don't you come up with me and learn my trade, there's more money in it." So he got into the business, learned about it, liked it, moved to another firm and learned some more. Then the bloke that owned the business went over to South Africa to start the same sort of firm there and left him in charge here. Now he's buying out that bloke in South Africa.'

The 'older friend', in that case, is twenty-one. It's not difficult to see how these examples encourage school 'failures', particularly when the people they admire give them their first work-experience. In this case it was a Saturday job. It makes the school 'failure' feel that there is really an opportunity to start afresh, and we have already noted that the statutory services sometimes give him a feeling that his past is following him around. Notice the informal job-getting network which involves 'this bloke said to him' and 'having a word with one of the gaffers.' It is very direct, and it is very different from the Careers Office. And these contacts do produce jobs.

Parents can play a similar role — if they are themselves employed. This 'unofficial' route to work is closed to those whose parents are unemployed. The next speaker has two older brothers, who both work in the same construction firm as their father:

> 'My Dad is the sort of bloke who never lets you have your own
> opinion, he never gives you a chance to speak. He pushed my
> eldest brother into brick-laying. When he left school he weren't
> sure what he wanted to do, but now he enjoys it, now he's been
> through tech. My other brother didn't know what he wanted to
> do either — first the army, then the police. So my Dad says,
> 'Right, you'll do what I want you to do.' So now he's a painter
> and decorator with the same firm as my Dad, and he enjoys it,
> but he feels it's not the best he could be doing. Now me, *I'm*
> going to choose what *I* want to do.'

This is the drawback, of course. It's yet more provision, in a way, if
your Dad fixes you up at his firm, and even though it can make life
easier, a school-leaver sometimes baulks at the reinforcement of his
'child' status. Young people know quite well that their parents are
worried about the publicised youth unemployment problem, and
this worry translates into nagging and arguments at home:

> 'They get moody when I don't seem to get a job anywhere . . .
> You parents don't know it's so hard. They say, "Go out and look
> for a job" — but there aren't any.'

We heard many young people complain like this young woman.
But sometimes their parents did seem justified in their nagging.
This speaker told us that she had 'tried for about forty jobs'. In fact,
we discovered that she had only written application letters and
attended interview for two, in several months. By 'tried', she meant
that she'd read a job description, recognised or assumed she'd no
chance, and therefore felt as though she'd actually applied and
been rejected. Maybe this looks like sheer laziness — it did to her
mother and father. It seemed to us to come from a desperate lack of
confidence, and fear of failing, yet again, to get a job. Rather than
stand up and take the fire, this girl decided for herself that she
wasn't good enough, and ducked out before anyone else could
reinforce her appalling lack of self-esteem.

It is hard for parents to repair this lack of confidence, or even to
observe it, since it is the sort of thing that is clearer to strangers than
to those who live close to it. On several occasions we interviewed
young people together with their parents, and in every case the
parents took over the interview. They often exhibited a lack of
knowledge of the 'system' and the precise problem facing their
children, and were as painfully confused about what to do

themselves.

Unfortunately it is often the parents of our 'bottom 30%' who are themselves least well-equipped to help their children understand the morass in which they find themselves at sixteen. Their knowledge of the possibilities open is poor, and this is understandable, given the complexities of the whole business. It is when this support fails them that school-leavers need the 'older friend' or 'adult support' which teachers, youth workers, career officers, purport to supply. But there is something that the 'older friend' shares with all friends, a fundamental feature — you choose him or her yourself.

Non-professional — but skilled

Over the past years we have noticed that the field of 'youth work', in its broadest sense, often includes adults who might best be described as 'eccentric'. It's rather unsatisfactory to lump these highly individual people under one heading, since their singularity is their chief characteristic. But they range from titled ladies who set up their own schemes for young people, to the man who lives on unemployment benefit and runs successful motor-cycle tuition classes. These people share a deep interest in the young and an inability to work with them in an institutional context. Perhaps we can best do them justice by giving a picture of one, a man who runs a day-centre for unemployed young people, not far from London. He told us how he first got involved.

'I was injured and on a pension, and for five years I looked after my own daughter while my wife was working. After my daughter went to school I found myself absolutely with nothing, and the house was closing in on me. And in the area where I lived there was a lot of little urchins doing damages, and breaking windows and uprooting trees. So I took them, one by one, and as a group, fishing, shooting, showing them the woods, teaching them what they can eat, how they can survive . . . Then one day a social worker came along and said: "I've heard so much about you, would you work with me in the social services?" Said "I can't offer you very much, but would you work as a volunteer for me, looking after children that have been in a problem family, have been in front of the courts." And I jumped into it with both feet . . . Then I noticed that there were too many unemployed young people lying about town. Some were creating trouble, and so I decided to open a place like this. Naturally I couldn't do it on my own. I had a friend and I exposed the idea to him, and he caught like wild-fire. And he, slowly and gently, pulled in other people that were interested, and we formed a working committee. We worked a year, just to make up a constitution and what the place was supposed to be used for. And we kept going for too long, and nothing was done. Here are a pile of papers, and we haven't yet decided what to do. I said, "Put your money where your mouth is!" So I put my hand in my pocket, took ten pounds I could ill afford to give, and put them on the table. And I said "Each one of you contribute." Taken in that way they couldn't very well refuse . . . That was £110.'

So they got a building, did it up, raised funds. And the man who began it now says that he 'gets the young people jobs'. How?

'You see, I receive lists of jobs from the Job Centre. I have a link there, a link that I have made with a young man who is very interested and, I should say, absolutely realistic about things. I write a letter and say "Right, go and see Chris, he will help you." If there is a job for their abilities, Chris will help. Personal contact is very important, but those contacts have taken a long time to establish.'

Where does that differ from the system that faces the school-leaver anyway? Isn't this man just an amateur careers officer? In fact, that is exactly what he is, but a 'Careers Officer' with a difference, based in a little terraced house which is called a 'day-centre', and available to listen to all kinds of problems. He is flamboyantly dressed, expansive of speech and gesture, and he catches the imagination of the young people who come to him.

'My role is to show them the necessity to keep their pecker up, to provide them with enough guts to go on and ability to keep their spirits up. And more and more I find myself in the role of having to find them abodes when father or mother throw them on the roads. So many kids are getting turned out from home that I am thinking of opening a hostel — my feelers are already out. If they apply for a job and have no fixed abode, they cannot get a job.'

We asked this man about his relationship with the statutory services, since he comes into contact with education, careers, social services, probation and after-care and other departments:

'They always think I'm an interloper. But I tell them, "You have outlines set to you by your job, that you have to stick to, even if you disagree." I don't have that kind of anchor on my feet. Nobody can sack me or make me lose my job. But I don't criticise the way they operate, because if I did it would be a stone around my neck. What I say is this: "I will work parallel with you. What you do wrong, I will straight; what I do wrong, you will straight." They refer kids to me now, that is what we have achieved. But I don't take no for an answer. I don't stop when they say to me "Stop".'

One user of the day centre said: 'He's really great — a real case.' We have seen many other 'characters' like this working with young people. They are very good at it.

Many young people told us that 'being treated as an adult' is important to them at work, and this affects the decisions they make about jobs. This young man was interviewed while he was unemployed:

'*What would you really like to be?*
A driver — lorries. Because I worked in the wholesale market for a time when I left school and I used to go out with some of the drivers on the lorries, delivering and that, and it seemed a good job. The drivers were good friends. I had dinner with them some days, when we worked late. We'd start about 5.30 in the morning and work till one or three, and we used to have a cup of tea and eat together. They treated me like their own age.'

And a girl said:

'You can learn things from anybody, not just teachers. They might be more useful. It's not like history — that's all about things that have happened, there's nothing you can do about it.'

To sum up the influence of non-official advisers and supporters of the young school leaver, one could say that they make young people feel there is something 'you can do about it'. They help to overcome the feeling that young people often have that they are victims.

So there are available, to some young people, sources of friendship, help, advice and support which, although untrained and sometimes poorly informed, nevertheless help them to find and keep work, or to cope with unemployment. These sources can, for some young people, be more effective than the professionals appointed to provide precisely this friendship, help, advice and support.

As we have seen, these people, these sources, are to be found here and there in the cracks between all the various institutions which comprise the youth suffocation business. Importantly they are found *within* work (where sympathetic working adult colleagues can, at best, be both 'real' teachers and experienced advisers), *around* it (where friends, family and odd 'cranks' provide friendly and informal help and advice on finding jobs), and *outside* it (where the same kinds of people help young people cope with unemployment and help them break out of it). Our conclusion, overall, is that these people, these experienced, 'first hand' sources of knowledge and advice are an important yet entirely undervalued aspect of continuing, 'community' education. They *must* be revalued, and the challenge is to do that without institutionalising them and without further eroding the need and ability of young people to do things on their own, in a self-reliant way. The 'Just the Job' counsellors show one way to do it. Within the working environment there seems to be a great deal of sense in the 'industrial coach' idea proposed and presently being developed by the Grubb Institute (John Bazalgette, *School Life and Work Life*). There seems to be just as great a need and potential for strengthening and revaluing the ways in which all those many sources of help, advice and knowledge contribute in, around and outside not just the work and work finding environments, but the education and 'youth work' environments, too. But all these 'alternatives', as we have tended to call them, presently operate as an unofficial and largely unrecognised fringe around the official systems, which greedily consume pretty well every penny that's available. The alternatives do not only have to battle for money, they then have to battle to avoid being merely taken over and stripped of their main asset: their difference. All that takes a lot of energy, and has defeated even the most hardened campaigners.

10   Government Programmes

It is noticeable that some of the new programmes for the young unemployed which the government has funded through the Manpower Services Commission do attract some staff who have this 'flair' for working with the young, but not always the qualifications which would allow them to do it professionally. And often they are people who eschew 'training', since they consider that what they can offer to young people owes more to instinct than certification.

These programmes have done a good deal to bring 'new' people into the business of helping the young unemployed. We have mentioned the MSC programmes already, but the picture needs completing. This is especially so since this kind of intervention raises several issues, particularly: are such measures for dealing with youth unemployment yet another institutional response, or can they broaden the responsibility for dealing with the problem?

The Youth Opportunities Programme costs a great deal of money, although in net terms this cost is smaller. It can even be said that, taking into account the savings on unemployment and supplementary benefit and also more hidden 'savings', it actually costs nothing at all. The aim of the programme is to provide young people with experience, skills and education that will improve their employability. We have already questioned whether this aim is realistic *now* — in those parts of the country where unemployment is already high — or in the immediate future, given the changing patterns of employment and shrinking numbers in some major sectors of employment. We have also noted the self-interests which exist among workers, employers and politicians, and the dilemmas which face a programme concerned with *education* as well as experience. And we have mentioned the responses made to the programme by some of the services which deal with young people, in particular further education and the youth service.

But there is one element that we've missed out so far, and this has generally gone unmarked, by those commenting on government measures to combat unemployment — yet it could well be their most significant aspect. The programme is based on the 'pot of gold' principle. The MSC says: 'We've got £200 million a year to spend, and we want to provide opportunities for about 250,000 young people per year; we propose to do this through a system of *sponsorship.*'

Sponsorship is an exciting idea, because it isn't exclusive, like institutional provision. It means that any responsible body can put up an idea and apply to be given money to take on young people. They may be employers, who can give young people industrial work experience; they may be local authorities, who want to carry out schemes for community benefit, from levelling slag heaps to personal community service work; they may be voluntary organis- ations, who do the same sort of thing; they may, really, be anybody. It is true to suspect that self-interest may well creep in here too, but admitting that and leaving it aside, what sponsorship does is to spread a responsibility widely. Its philosophy is closer to that of the Adult Literacy movement, which we have described, and far less close to bureaucratically minded institutional responses — like the National Health Service, for example. The question is whether it can stay like that.

It is worth measuring this programme for young people against the yard-sticks they have given us themselves. How varied are these opportunities? To what extent do they take account of the differences between individual young people, their needs and aspirations? The good news is this:

'. . . the . . . programme (YOP) . . . must be designed to meet the personal needs of individual unemployed young people as they seek to secure permanent employment ·. . .' *(Young People and Work)*, MSC.

This aim recognises only limited needs among the young people it seeks to touch, and those are the needs related to employability. Aside from this restriction, it does represent an important change in the theory of provision for the young. It says 'We will start from where young people are', rather than: 'How can we fit young people· into what we are doing?'

In practical terms this is demonstrated by the provision of different kinds of opportunities. The programme offers different kinds of training courses and different kinds of work experience, so it is not totally stuck in the 'this is the policy' rut of so much government provision. There are 'employment induction' and 'short industrial' courses, and work experience 'with employers', in 'community service', in 'workshop-based' commercial enterprises and on environmental and constructional 'projects'. Each of these different kinds of schemes, sponsored by various agencies, must meet certain criteria, criteria which are framed by the MSC to further the objective of meeting 'the personal needs of individual unemployed young people'. For example, there must be some educational element in the opportunities, and there must be proper support and counselling arrangements. All of which sounds all right; but incorporated in the programme are two glaring mistakes.

The first of these lies in the fact that sponsors must apply . . . Who judges the applications? Well, the £200 million is allocated to various areas of the country on the basis of need. The greater the youth unemployment in an area, the more that area gets, which is fair and reasonable. Each area has a special office and a committee of people drawn from various walks of life to oversee the spending of the money. The offices are staffed by a total of more than 700 civil servants. They do not know very much about young people or their needs. They are responsible to government ministers and, as far as the money is concerned, to the Treasury and the Exchequer. And the committees, or Areas Boards as they are known, are not composed of parents, young people, and others close to the problem, they are made up from people whose main interests are self-interests. They come from business, the unions, the professions, and if they have a personal concern with the predicament of the young unemployed, it generally derives from the chance that they have children in the age-group. Mostly the members of Area Boards are too old for this.

So the judges of applications for government funding under the new programmes are, at official level, inexperienced in the problems of young school-leavers, and the same applies at the committee level. And the Areas into which the programme divides the country for administrative purposes are remote from the detailed realities of the problem. There are only thirty or so of these units, and they have to cover a wide geographical area. So it looks as though the administration of this programme is remote, inexperienced and peppered with self-interests whose main concern is not young people. But so far, it is the best we have.

Since the encouragement of sponsorship is such an exciting thing to see a centralised government department doing, it is a pity that sponsorship is not firmly rooted in local initiative, local cooperation and local participation. If it were, it should be possible to do away with the bulk of those 700 administering civil servants. But comments on such suggestions are disdainful of the 'interference' such widespread participation would invite. As the man who runs the day-centre told us, there is a fear of the 'interloper'. Admittedly some of the new programmes are getting people like him to work in them, but the administrative structure means that they miss many opportunities to appeal to untapped energy in the community.

Then we should remember the young people whose need for help and opportunity is greatest when they leave school. They have been least well prepared by school, and often have the least ability to plug into the family-and-friends job-finding network, they live in areas where unemployment is highest. The new 'system' is hardly geared to them. Sponsors, with their own interests in mind, apply for money to run a scheme providing opportunities for the young unemployed to gain experience and learn. The application is considered and approved by people who are not experienced in the problems of the disadvantaged young, and who have their own interests to consider. They are also under political pressure to deliver numbers and to reduce the dole queues. In consequence they do not ask the prospective sponsor too many awkward questions about motivation for establishing schemes, nor do they set too many awkward conditions on the granting of the funding. The MSC, although anxious to ensure that 'the personal needs of individual unemployed young people' are met, and including the less able in that group, does not instruct sponsors as to *who* they should recruit. Nor do the Careers and Employment Services. So sponsors can recruit who they want. And, like any employer, they will choose the best avaialable. Who can blame them? They have to consider their own interests. That is why sponsoring employers can boast of success rates of the order of 80% and more of the young people they take on work experience schemes finding work. And that is also why many places on schemes which have been 'approved' are not actually filled. Sponsors want the best that is available, and often that's not the young person with the greatest need.

The problem of inexperience among the administrators of the government programmes would seem easily solved. Why not recruit some people who have appropriate experience of working with young people? The answer we are always given to this question is that the Civil Service Unions will not have 'outsiders' doing work which they feel should be done by their members. These are the same unions which will not allow government departments to sponsor work experience schemes under the Youth Opportunities Programme. The reasons are that it might threaten the rights of existing workers and that 'the money should be spent to take on more permanent staff' — who would not be young, unqualified and inexperienced, of course. This is a good example of worker self-interest. It is attitudes like these which prevent the development of experience among administrators of programmes like these. This sets off a chain reaction of mistakes in the approval of applications for funding, so that there is often a wrong decision, taken within the wrong structures, on the wrong criteria.

There are three stages which an approach to youth unemployment, that aims to involve the whole community, can go through. First there is the sponsorship idea. In a locality it should be possible to adopt a planned approach, so that what the sponsor aims to provide is based on the total 'need' of the area; a developmental approach, so that there will be ways to fill in the gaps where sponsors do not come forward, or where they cannot meet the demands of the needs of young people, or cannot satisfy the government's 'criteria'. The locality must determine the right *scale* of approach.

Then it is essential that sponsors and all participants work together in a collective way, because if they do not, then whatever they set up for young people will be as fragmented as all the other services they experience. And it is only through a collective approach that there will be a chance of neutralising all the self-interests that are at work, and of allowing young people to move from one kind of experience to another, to sample, to broaden their knowledge, to find a milieu which suits them. For many young people, 'meeting needs' simply means 'offering choice'.

The third stage must be when this collective response begins to involve itself with, and work in concert with those other services, individuals and actions, themselves collective, individual and institutional, which affect young people. In so doing, there must be a well-tuned awareness of the danger of ending up with some kind of super-institution.

At present the measures to deal with youth unemployment are getting stuck around the first stage. There are voluntary organisations and local authorities who avoid the mire and get local people together with a combination of imaginative catalysis and some banging together of heads. But these successes are in spite of inexperience and self-interest, and it is very hard work to achieve them.

Sponsors, as we have mentioned, have to meet some fairly basic criteria if they are to get funding for their schemes. As time goes on, these criteria become more sophisticated. Under the earlier Job Creation Programme the aim was simple: to create temporary 'worthwhile' jobs of 'social and community benefit'. There was no 'youth' orientation and no bias towards the 'unqualified'. So the more self-interested motivations of sponsors towards fitting themselves up with cheap, but well-qualified labour, flourished. There was teaching for unemployed teachers, and research for unemployed graduates; public work schemes for hard-up local authorities, extra staff for hard-pressed voluntary organisations. It was crude, but statistically effective.

But with the 'individual need' orientation of the new programmes have come new criteria, for proper counselling and educational arrangements, and for recruiting only young people. To meet these criteria many sponsors have found it *necessary* to work with other people and organisations which have the necessary experience. The beginnings of partnership and collective administrative arrangements emerged. In Bristol, for example, the WRVS, sponsoring community service work experience, got together with the local further education college, sponsoring assessment and training courses; they pulled in local youth workers, the Careers Service, a voluntary organisation concerned with young people on probation, the local authority . . . But some individuals and small organisations who work closely with young people found that, though in a good position to respond to individual needs, they could not meet the criteria. Many small voluntary and community groups lacked the resources and the required experience, many statutory youth workers could not take initiatives without approval from their 'superiors'. And sometimes what small organisations wanted to do was beyond the knowledge and experience of the less experienced people who administered the scheme.

Once approved, however, schemes could recruit adult staff to manage, supervise, counsel and teach: to do many things which existing institutions had always thought to be *their* preserve. The result is that for the first time many young people are finding themselves with an adult who can give them *first-hand* experience and advice; people who regard them, at best, as work-mates, rather than clients; at worst as work-mates as well as 'clients'. But not as *children*.

This kind of relationship is not important to young people alone. The adults themselves find it useful and more manageable than the pupil-teacher relationship. This man is a supervisor on a scheme for young unemployed people:

'I get on well with young people, but probably not so well now as I did in my younger day, because you have a different relationship with them and they look upon you differently. When you have the energy and are still a little bit carefree, you can go along with the kids and they can see this. They will relate to older people as well as younger people, but it's a different type of relationship. They have some respect for experience and age, they don't fool around as much with the older person. The last thing a kid wants to be told is what's good for him. He wants to find out for himself what's good for him.'

And he went on:

'I like young people — they are the life of the country, they are the people who are going to make the future of this country. Who knows what they'll become — and a lot of the guidance we give them now will determine what they'll become later. They are going through an age now, from the time they leave school until they are eighteen or so, when they are going to try a lot of things to see what they can do and what they can get away without doing. We are taking them away from a lot of things they know when they come here, and you can see, physically, kids grow up, in the way they carry themselves, the way they speak. After about nine weeks they change considerably and you're sorry to see them go. There are a lot who aren't confident when they come here, and you have to build that up. Confidence is having the ability to do something that will be useful.'

Community Industry, a small, national job creating scheme began before any of the MSC programmes, and it made use of this idea: giving skilled adult workers the additional role of friend and adviser to young working colleagues. Many of the new MSC schemes were small, which allowed the closeness of contact which developed these relationships. Naturally these adults often need some rudimentary training, but it would be a pity if this were carried to the extreme of professional qualification. The institutional dangers are there. But it is interesting to see how the professionals who have always seen the 'friend and adviser' role as their own 'patch', have viewed this encouraging development with nervous reservation.

So these new government-funded programmes contain good

things and bad things. The experience that young people can get on them is often more limited than it should be. They cannot stay on a scheme for more than a year and in reality many can only stay for a few weeks. The schemes which are funded through the programmes may well not provide enough places of the right kind of quality for the 'less able'. And it is necessary to look beyond 'employability' as the sole objective of such measures. This is not only because unemployment is growing, but because the jobs many young people — the less able in particular — will eventually get are not the most dignified or satisfying start to adult life. Though these programmes may avoid institutionalisation, because the sponsorship method means that all sorts of different people are continually striving to make sure that they do, yet it will still be easy for them to fall into the familiar "provision" attitude.

And so we return to the question we began with. What are young people for? Simply to be made fit for work?

11 The Planned Shape of Things to Come?

'It's hard to grow up when there isn't enough man's work. There is "nearly full employment" (with highly significant exceptions), but there get to be fewer jobs that are necessary or unquestionably useful; that require energy and draw on one's best capacities; and that can be done keeping one's honour and dignity.'
(Paul Goodman, *Growing Up Absurd*)

There is little honour and dignity in being treated as a child up to and even beyond the age of sixteen. There is little honour and dignity in being an unemployment statistic, or being a wage-slave in a job you hate, or being a helpless client in need of paternal assistance. But it is in the interests of adults to keep things this way.

It is a wasteful way to treat young people, and the problems it causes cannot be properly dealt with by embellishing adult-dominated, professionally-certificated institutions with more help, more care, more treatment for the clients. This problem is larger than that implied by the phrase 'school-to-work transition', and answers to it must be more fundamental than 'school-industry links', 'work experience', or national government programmes. This is not the sort of problem where real solutions can be *bought*.

National 'community' service

But purchasable solutions are periodically mooted. One is the idea of national "community" service. The MSC survey of young unemployed people asked:

'Would you be willing to spend 6-12 months doing community work (e.g. taking care of children, doing outdoor work or helping old and disabled people) while being paid at unemployment benefit level?'

69% of girls and 43% of boys answered 'Yes'.

The lobby pushing for the introduction of such a scheme contains a strange alliance of those who feel that young people owe a debt to the society which has raised them, and those who feel that young people will benefit from the experience, even if it is enforced. The latter remember the comments of those who did national military service and said afterwards that it broadened their horizons, taught them a trade, brought them into contact with a lot of other people, 'rubbed the corners off'. Add to this the 'social doom' arguments, which predict the collapse of public services unless an army of youth is mobilised, and the people who find that the suggestion 'National Service' gets them a big hand on 'Any Questions?'. The result is an oddly assorted collection.

Increasingly the arguments have been for a 'targeted' programme, aimed at those who stayed on at school reluctantly when the leaving age was raised. This misses the point that it may well be the academic achievers who *need* the broadening experience. Elsewhere other 'targeted' groups for community service have emerged. Under the Community Service Order Scheme offenders can be sentenced to up to 240 hours of community service, and young people deemed 'at risk' can be diverted from the crimes they may commit by community service undertaken as part of an 'intermediate treatment' scheme operated by social services departments. The consequence of its use as a response to various 'problems' has made community service a kind of "badge of failure", and a national community service scheme is liable to reinforce this reputation.

There is a danger in talking about national community service, voluntary or compulsory as a single solution to the needs of young people. There is a great variation in their needs, aspirations and privileges, which make this a far more complicated issue. If national community service were boiled down to some period, between school and work, or school and higher education, then the possibility of doing it at other times would be lost. And the effect of the experience on the parallel education processes would be lost too.

The "16-18 institution"

All the signs at present point to another 'catch-all' solution. This is the extension of educational provision in a concerted way from 16 to 18. This doesn't mean that the school leaving age is likely to be raised. Rather, the development of special programmes and further education, with the parallel development of incentives and attractions to young people to opt for them, will have the effect of extending the 'education-leaving age'. These incentives will be both financial and also offered as more attractive than the alternative, boring, unsatisfying job. Eventually this will be represented at a national level by the establishment of a Minister for Education and Training, ending the split between MSC work-based education and training schemes, and DES further education and youth services. All sixteen-year-olds will receive a standardised allowance, as they already do on MSC schemes. Sixth formers and further education students will follow. There will be a great deal of debate about means tests and fairness. It will cost a great deal of money, which is why the 1979 election may put it all off for a while. But it will mean (and this is what makes it attractive to most shades of political opinion) that 16-18-year-olds can be excluded from unemployment statistics altogether. Lower retirement ages will take a slice off the other end of the statistics, and we'll all learn to live with high unemployment that way: by conveniently forgetting that much of it exists. Once we have pensioned off the inexperienced young and the redundant old, we will share out what's left in the middle with shorter working weeks, and perhaps manage to magic unemployment away completely. Those who predict 6 million unemployed by the end of the century forget how sharp we are at adapting, and how quick to forget. The youth education/training programmes will provide controlled entries into the labour force, by smoothing out peaks and troughs caused by many young people leaving school at two or three particular points in the year. It will also neatly homogenise the young people, and remove that distinction between 'unemployed young people' and the rest. That way the problem will be dealt with and the self-interests left untouched, with the odd 'great' debate about education cropping up every few years.

If this sounds fanciful, it is nevertheless presaged by the report of an independent working party set up recently by the Northern Ireland education minister, Lord Melchett:

'All 16 to 18 year olds in Northern Ireland should be found jobs or given financial support to continue their education . . . The report says that the plan would not create jobs but would make it possible to dispense with the present emergency measures: "What is not needed, in our view, is an ill-assorted collection of short-term remedial programmes, with a mainly cosmetic effect, obscuring the fundamental issue". The working party say a full education and training programme for all 16-18 year olds in Great Britain could be hampered by the cost, but it was a more

practical proposal in Northern Ireland . . .'
(*Guardian,* October 1978)

This proposed programme would be:

'. . . a comprehensive scheme of education and training for all up
to 18. Not, it should hastily be added, a longer period of
compulsory education. Rather, the report is about the
opportunities which can be offered, and the incentives which can
be held out, so that, as the notion of juvenile unemployment fast
disappears, it can be replaced by an integrated and comprehensive programme of secondary and further education, industrial
training and vocational preparation . . . not an emergency
response to temporary unemployment but . . . a way of meeting
long-term needs. It is not concerned with stop-gaps for school
leavers but an articulated programme for the full two years
following the minimum leaving age . . .'
(*Times Educational Supplement,* October 1978)

Some suggestions in this report confirmed our scepticism about
'catch all' ideas for 16-18 year olds. One was that money now being
spent on 'emergency measures' for the young unemployed in
Northern Ireland — where there is a YOP similar to the MSC
programmes — might be better used to provide attendance grants
to make sure that less able 14 and 15 year olds come to school!
There would be an 'attainment test' at 15, with those who fail
having to stay on and take it again. Those who failed yet again
would be offered financial incentive to stay on and try yet again!
The report suggests that young people who are offered jobs should
not be allowed to leave school early.

There are many advantages to more coherent approaches to
education and training (whether work- or institution-based). For
example, it would enable young people who gain motivation, often
for the first time, from work experience or work, to pursue courses
of study without difficulty and financial hardship. The present
short length of stay in the MSC youth programme, plus the
financial penalties of going back to school or college, make such
courses of action impossible for many young people. There are
other advantages to such coherence, in, say, ensuring within a wide
range of opportunities that those who have been failed by school get
a better chance. But it is wrong to pretend that this need only
assumes importance between the ages of 16 and 18. And to pretend
that a new super-institutional approach will meet this need, misses

the importance and potential of wider participation and involvement.

The problem of payment

Another difficulty with such schemes is that there is no relationship between input and output. If you are making an input into a system, whether you are making a product or performing a service, you have the right (which you may decline if you want to) to get something in return, for your input has a value. You are paid, in other words, and vice versa. Modern welfare systems confuse the simplicity of this equation, but only slightly. Up to the day on which you leave school, you get the output, but you don't have to pay the teacher who makes the input. The taxpayer does that, your mum and dad are doing it for you. They pay indirectly unless you go to a fee-paying school, when they pay directly by cheque. But if all 16-18 year olds get some form of payment, regardless of whether they are "work experiencing" or learning, or training, what is that payment *for?* Is it a benefit to stay alive, a grant or allowance to pay your bills, or an output wage as a reward for what you are putting in?

The young person on an MSC scheme gets an *allowance* and he is called a *trainee*. Yet if he's in a workshop he is making and selling things, if he's on a project doing community service work, he's providing needed services. So he's *working* for much of the time and yet by name (trainee) and by payment (allowance) he *isn't* a worker. And what does incentive mean in all this?

Does it mean that we are still in a make-believe world, a world where kids get pocket-money because they've been good, or because they've helped Mummy with the shopping? Even though they may be eighteen years old? Blurring the distinctions between inputs, outputs, handouts and pacifiers is an affront to the honour and dignity of young people and a dishonest comment on their worth and potential. These distinctions should be made clear: *wages* for work, *grants* for education, which could be called *allowances* for training, and *benefit*, or some better word, if you are unable to do any of those things. The grant/allowance is not pay for the education and training, it is a benefit to enable you to live in a situation where you make no input and therefore get no output. It should depend on your circumstances — for example, on whether you have others to support and on whether you are a full-time student or trainee, for you may be working for wages at the same time.

Young people who want to leave school at the earliest possible opportunity all say that they want to earn money. 'You can't do anything if you don't have some money' is a common comment. However, the amount of money you get on the dole is not considered sufficient for 'doing' anything. When we suggested that school would be more attractive if there was an 'incentive' for staying there, this was greeted with derision. Among early leavers this is not a sufficient bribe to make them put up with the other things they dislike about school. However, at earlier stages in their school life, pupils did suggest, quite often, that school would be more palatable if you got paid for attending.

'Plenty more people would come all the time if they got paid. You wouldn't get so much truanting.'

Presence at school, of course, does not mean more maturity, better examination results. It does mean that there are fewer kids on the streets when they should be at school. And that is neat and tidy.

12 Missing Ingredients — Risk, Role and Reality

Unlike Lord Melchett's working party, we would propose that young people should be allowed, indeed, encouraged, to vary their educational diet at 13 years. This doesn't mean lowering the school or education-leaving age. But from that age onwards, young people should, if they can, and if they so choose, begin to spend part of their time working, or simply being away from education, or continuing education, in an entirely different environment. It seems reasonable to suggest that at 13 this would be for no more than one day a week, at 14, two days a week, and at 15 no more than three days a week. But such experience need not and should not simply take the form of 'days a week'. Some young people might choose to aggregate them and have a week, a month, or even a year out of the mainstream.

When young people talk about truancy, they frequently say they begin to do it around the age of thirteen or fourteen.

'I never went to school much, I just didn't like school. I couldn't stay at home, because my mother didn't allow me to stop off, you know. I just fooled around. It wasn't boring, no. I was with my mates. If I was on my way to school and I looked at my timetable and found that I had something I didn't like, I just didn't go.

When did you start to dislike going to school?
I can't remember. It was about the third year that I started drifting away. I didn't take any exams at all. I didn't like the teachers at all. All that teachers bother with, they only bother with the ones they think will pass, and the other ones, that are a bit slow — I'm not slow but — they just didn't bother with. They weren't interested in me because I took time off.'

That speaker is now 'working' — on a government-funded work experience scheme.

Some schools have developed work experience or community service to the point where it would be a small step to bring current practice into line with our proposal. But it is a pity that such practice is confined at present to those young people who do not fit the school's idea of 'normality'. This teacher is responsible for a special unit within a school for young people with 'emotional disturbances'. Work experience is a key part of their routine:

'Usually the kids start one day a week, and then, ideally, we would move up to three or four days a week, especially if there's a chance of getting a job at that place at the end of the year. If there's not, the case has to be decided on its own merits. John, here, did one day, then he wanted to do two, now he's doing three, although there's not a job at the end of this placement for him, at this particular work. So we are trying to get interviews at suitable places that he wants to work at in town. We never tell the kids that there'll be a job at the end of a placement. It's not aimed at that, anyway, it's aimed to show them that work is different from school. There are different people to relate to, possibly in a harsher regime than they have experienced at school. There's one lad who, next week, will be doing five days work experience until he leaves school, because the job has been promised to him when he leaves, so we won't see him again.'

This girl was pointing in the same direction:

'Kids in school, they should persuade them to find out what they want to do by the time they're in their third year — then they pick the subjects that's got something to do with what they're going to do.'

So this is not a proposal intended to do for truancy what Lord Melchett's working party hope to do to juvenile unemployment — sweep it out of sight. It is put forward in recognition of things which our present educational system cannot provide, things which are important for growing up, for gaining honour and dignity and which offer a clearer sight of the question: 'What are young people for?' But such a change would necessitate wholesale overhaul of our attitudes to, and ways of working with, young people. It would mean the break-up of much of the youth suffocation business; it would necessitate major changes in the structures of the services to young people which make up this business; and far greater debates than the ones we have right now.

If young people are to grow up, to become part of our adult society — and there is an inevitability about that — we must make a number of experiences and opportunities available to them. Most important, they must have a chance to ease themselves into the adult world, rather than be kept out of it until some belated day of reckoning which is chosen by adults. Many societies which we call 'primitive' and 'under-developed' have methods of entry and initiation firmly established in their cultural life — so firmly it is easy to overlook their importance. They are methods which do not overlook the clear natural and physical markers of adulthood. These natural signposts are totally ignored by our education system, 11 years being generally rather young, 16 too old. An eighteen-year-old is a man or woman in every physical sense, whatever part of the world he or she lives in.

But when life is about survival and subsistence it is easy to see that young people have a role. The smallest carry babies, fetch water, hoe the land, keep the goats. The flavour of this sort of childhood is available in novels by East and West African authors and is well-described in the first part of Alex Haley's *Roots*. For the most part our 'non-primitive' lives are not about survival. We have baby buggies, the water comes in pipes and milk is delivered to the doorstep. We replace the goats with pet kittens and hamsters, and a million silly ideas from Blue Peter help to while away youthful years.

Where survival is still the name of the game in this country, on the land or in the decaying cities, young people are attracted to it, attracted to its risks, its realism and the roles they can play in it. Very often they are forced to overcome barriers of adult protection and paternalism to get there. And once they do, they are allowed to participate only in limited areas, defined by modern institutions and by law.

We consider that these '3 R's' are central to any discussion about education reform: risk, role and realism. They are as relevant to the needs of young people as those more familiar '3 R's', taught in the class-room. But the class-room does not and cannot provide them, although many teachers recognise the need for them. One important way of realising and meeting this need is through community service in school. Like allowing young people out of the class-room into situations which can be frightening — like a ward of severely sub-normal patients in a hospital, which assaults every sensibility; where they are needed — because there will never be enough hands and time and kindness to service a ward like that; and where the situation is not a game — however much the adult world likes to go about its business and pretend that such places do not exist. There are other elements of existing practice which, with a little imagination, can be vehicles for such experience.

Experiments in alternative approaches to education which are not smothered by the institutional takeover, often try to build such experiences into their practice. But even in an ordinary school, there are 'trips'.

Many teachers who have organised 'trips', trips of a rugged and demanding nature, make similar comments when they return. They have seen new dimensions to their pupils. An opportunity was provided for hidden qualities to emerge, for the discussion of issues in an informal setting, for ossified roles of teacher and pupil to change. It's at these times that teachers sometimes listen and young people relax enough to tell. But this kind of thing tends to be seen as an 'occasional extra', a luxury on the fringe of education, and, of course, it has to be paid for. But why should it be that way round? Why not have the trips as the free part, the part the tax-payer pays for, and pay extra for the classes? Probably because nobody would pay . . . We have sailed on canal barges with young people, lived in deserts and struggled up the Pennine Way with them, fighting for survival, exercising cunning and initiative to camp near a pub each night, sharing duties, being a group of equals. We have no doubt of the benefit of this kind of risk and realism and the value of the roles which emerge from it. Who cooks? Who washes? Who carries the heaviest load? Who needs help because his feet are sore?

Two teachers at a school in California were in this position. One was taking young people on wild-water river trips at weekends, the other was taking them back-packing and climbing in the mountains. They observed the impact on the young people who came. A chance conversation in the staff-room revealed that they were coming to similar conclusions, and together they wrote a proposal for a 'school within a school'. They wanted to provide students with an opportunity to learn at first-hand in the environment, to get to know their own strengths and weaknesses; to develop the former and overcome the latter; to gain pleasure and satisfaction from serving others; to prepare for life and work in society. The Principal of their high school accepted the proposal. The school was in a depressed area and the two teachers could see numbers of students getting by in school by being stoned out of their minds, others dropping out and never 'graduating'. When the 'school within a school' was set up, students could opt to join it for half a school year. It was called 'On Location'.

'On Location' courses had several parts. First, there were three two-week long camping trips, all of a very arduous nature: pack-packing and camping in the Sierra Nevada, in the coastal mountains around Big Sur, in the desolate wilderness of Death Valley. Between these trips came community service projects, with students working as individuals in local institutions for the physically and mentally handicapped, teaching and tutoring in primary schools and so on. Then there was a period of work in a job which the student chose and which the teachers helped to make possible.

Observing the young people on this course, we noticed that our '3 R's' found practical expression in the things they were doing. On the trips, the young people were organising themselves, for cooking, for example, for sharing other responsibilities and for making decisions and rules of behaviour. We were interested to see how well this was done. One of the problems that taxes the staff-meetings at many a liberal comprehensive school in this country is *names!* Should pupils call teachers by first names, or should some pupils . . . or does this undermine the pupil/teacher relationship . . . Since we had sat in on many a discussion of this kind, we were bowled over by the simplicity of the solution at 'On Location'. At a first course meeting, the two teachers and 40 odd students simply said the name by which they would like to be known. For one of the teachers, this was his first name, for the other, this was his surname — without the Mr.

There has been a good deal of talk recently about political education, with the Department of Education and Science awarding grants to national youth organisations to investigate how this can be purveyed. At 'On Location' political education is practical and necessary. There are decisions to be made about priorities, roles and laws, and these must provide a framework for the course to operate. This is very real politics, and although it seems far from parties and Senate, Hill and House, it nevertheless provides a very real insight into organisation and the need for it. The difficulties and problems which arose for the young people we saw were not all of their own-making. They had to find ways of coping with the academic 'credit' system of American high schools, with participants disillusioned and frustrated by the experiences of years of boredom and authority-fighting. But they were managing to do it, and the project survives to this day, now expanded to include all the schools in an area.

Risk

It's important to be clear about the words we are using. Risk means finding opportunities which *make demands* upon individual young people. Traditionally we have come to associate risk with physical challenges. Most people need these in some form or other. Some of them climb mountains, others seek risks nearer home, on the highway, in the streets, in confrontation. The Outward Bound idea is a good one, but it is not the only way to develop character and initiative, self-reliance and self-confidence. It's all very well to invent more and more challenging situations — the Eiger in summer, the Eiger in winter, the Eiger feet first, without shoes and so on. But *emotional* risks are found in other circumstances. And what one person takes in their stride, another has to face as an emotional risk.

When we have listened to young people talking about community service experiences, occasionally we have heard how the right level of risk has been faced by an individual. To enable this balance to occur, there has to be great sensitivity among those who set it up. Actually, this is often not the case, and the examples we have seen, where risk has been at the right level for the young person experiencing it, have often come about by chance. Here is a teacher who described how one experience came about in this way:

'A couple of years ago I had a girl who was a total failure in school . . . She was totally isolated. She'd be polite when I spoke to her, but otherwise I never had a spontaneous communication from her. I was worried about how she'd make out . . . We were working down at the day-care centre, playing dominoes and cards with these elderly people, many of them disabled. I turned round to wave the pupils in, this girl several paces behind. The others looked round, took an elderly person each, sat down, introduced themselves and so on. (The girl) stood in the middle of the floor. There was only one chap left, who'd obviously had a severe stroke, one side of his mouth being quite paralysed, one arm useless. He was the only one left. His jaw sagged, he drooled at the mouth. The others had avoided him. The girl went over to him and sat down . . . for five weeks I watched that pair play draughts without exchanging a word. One week she was off and that old man cried . . .'

We have watched one group of young people working with severely handicapped and subnormal children in a session which they call 'drama therapy'. The aim is to develop powers of communication and response in the children. They acted out stories, made noises, charged around, exercised limbs. The atmosphere was tense, challenging and very demanding, and what was going on was clearly very hard work. The young people involved had been helped by a friendly local drama teacher, who instructed them in necessary techniques. But in the session that we watched, nobody interfered. Professional staff at the home where they were working left them to it, trusting their good sense and ability. Their teacher stayed at home. The sessions go on regularly, every week, and they are moving and challenging to watch. It is clear from work like this that, after receiving the right kind of help, young people can grow up through experiences on their own. But support should be around for the times when they get stuck.

'I have a list of thirty or forty local employers, all of whom take kids, or are prepared to take kids on work experience. They range from very small, one-man concerns, like butchers, to places like Chryslers. I collected that list myself mostly and it's evolved over the years. One boy works at a local supermarket, so it was very easy to pop in and ask them whether they were prepared to take part in a work experience scheme. Other kids have said "My friend's Dad works at such and such a place" so I've contacted them.'

Needless to say, the teacher himself has taken something of a risk, since he is always in danger of a rebuff from the people he asks to help. He also has to put in quite a bit of extra work in finding the opportunities, and support while the kids are in them:

'When we think a kid is mature enough and succeeding at various things we tell him what is available for him. If there is a kid who is hell-bent on being a mechanic, there is no point in putting him in a bakery or a shop. Sometimes it is enough that they should have experience of work. I have to see the guy at the firm and sell the scheme to him, tell him about the kid and sell the kid to him. Make sure the insurance and the red tape are dealt with — that's time-consuming.

Then I take the kid down one morning and introduce him to the right people, and then he disappears into the bosom of the firm! That can be quite scary. I've taken boys to garages where there is a lot of noise, or a big supermarket, where there's a lot of activity. I can feel it in the kids, the nervousness, it is all completely new for them. But most of the boys will tell you that they can step out into work that much easier having tasted something of it, rather than leaving here — which is a very comfortable place — and straight down the careers office.'

The impact of the experience on the young people justifies the efforts this teacher is making:

> 'We've found that the majority of kids that have gone out to work, have come back to us and they look different, they look *physically* different even after one day. They've usually put in a hard day at work, they've got a lot of esteem from doing it, and that means they present themselves differently to us. It doesn't mean they haven't come back with problems they had before, they just seem to be growing up faster — which is lovely to see.'

Sometimes, when the question of risk and the young is debated, it is said that children cannot cope with such exposure, that they might be killed, or injured or deeply shocked, and that they might harm other people, because they are young, inexperienced and unused to these demands. Others say that childhood should be a joyful, happy time, and that it should not be ruined by the imposition of responsibilities like these. Young people themselves do not say such things. Even when they have had experiences which have been *too* demanding, they have learned from them, discovered their weaknesses as well as realised their talents. There are no risks in schools, and there would be no risks in a new super-institution for 16 to 18 year olds.

Role

The second R is role. We have observed that school offers no role to the young people in it, except as a part of prefect and monitorial systems. Unemployment is a classic state of being without role, at least in a society where employment is considered the norm. How can you have a useful function if you don't have a job? But some jobs hardly offer role, when they are mindless, boring, peripheral. What kind of useful contribution are you making in a job like *that?*

Many authorities are aghast when they see first-time job-seekers flitting from one job to another. They point to it as an example of the fickleness of young people, the inadequacy of careers and employment advice (and the need to strengthen it!), or the mismatch between the requirements of industry and the abilities and aspirations of young people. But our conclusions, based on the things young people have told us, are rather different. It seems that young people want to sample, and that in sampling they are looking, at first, for something which offers more satisfaction, more obvious usefulness, than boring and repetitive work. Eventually the realisation dawns for many that they are condemned to this sort of work. But job-changing is a hopeful clue to the fact that many young school-leavers still have hope. More important to a surprising majority than 'a good wage' is 'a satisfying job' or 'doing something worthwhile'.

It seems that we should offer young people roles from an early age. These would be positions of respect, positions of usefulness, positions where they have an obvious and *needed* part to play; positions where they are rewarded not just with money, but with gratitude, praise and respect. Saturday and part-time jobs can contain these rewards, but too often the work is low on pay and respect. Role is also potentially available through community service, since it is the caring industry that always needs more hands, and which can absorb help almost endlessly, provided, of course, we can find a way around the incumbent 'care-mongers'.

But, apart from the threat that it offers to our role, as adults, we must admit that the great drawback to providing roles for young people is the hard work that must be put in to set them up. Our experience is that there are many teachers and youth-workers who realise that young people need a role, and that they haven't got one because it suits the youth suffocation business that they shouldn't have one. But teachers and careers officers and youth workers who feel that way are caught in a professional net, which renders them powerless to open up the kind of possibilities that the two teachers in California explored.

The examples we quoted of young people at risk in drama therapy, or working with the elderly, are also examples of young people with roles. We have found many such examples of role-development through community service, even though the mechanisms which express the practice are often sterile. The community service element of the MSC's Youth Opportunities Programme represents the first chance the activity has had to operate on a properly-funded basis. But this scheme, too, is liable to find self-interests which divert young people away from real roles, into peripheral and undemanding fringe activities. Why does the development of role have to wait until the late age of 16, and why just for those young people who find themselves without a job?

Here are some examples of role and what it can mean to young people. The first speaker is fifteen, and still at school:

'Four years ago I was so shy, it was terrible. I think I've come out a lot more since I've been working here, meeting the mothers as well as the children. I know the mothers' names, they always say hello when I pass them in the street. They recognise me not just as a kid but as somebody who works at the playgroup and helps train their kids. They know that I do something.'

The next speaker is an organiser, and she is talking about a young person working on an environmental project:

'One boy who was there was slightly crippled, he couldn't read or write, he could just about write his name. The kids got on well with him at school to a certain extent, but he was the sort of form idiot. The teachers . . . realised he was one of those cases they couldn't help with. He went to the project, he was there for the full fortnight. They allowed him to go every day, because he wanted to work with wood. In the end he had sole possession of the portable bench, and he was sawing up tree roots. He had his sandwiches in his pocket and he ate them when he was hungry — he wouldn't stop for his dinner. He'd talk to you, but he just wouldn't stop work. I said "Don't you ever stop?" and he said "Never been so happy in my life". That project was worth it, if only for him. He was a changed lad, and the others had so much respect for him at the end of that fortnight, they really did.'

And while visiting elderly people is not everyone's idea of a useful role, these two young men from Liverpool pointed out that it was wrong to generalise:

'This one we go to at the moment is smashing. We sort of wash the dishes and tidy up in general and we talk and have cups of tea. We never used to get a cup of tea . . . But for all that it's hard work because we often clear up the house. She's got a couple of sons who live with her . . . a spastic son as well, so we have to help him, like. We both go every day, and there's still plenty to do. She can't always get about because she's very ill, and her sons are at work . . . When we are off school she always phones up school to see where we are, and she always asks to speak to the teacher to see where we are.'

Is that important to you?
Yes, she needs us. If we don't do the shopping she's got no way of getting it. She says to us, "Are you coming this afternoon? Are you coming tonight?" And if we say no, she says, "Can't you put it off and come here, like?"

Another young person told us about the experience he had with a mentally handicapped boy in hospital:

> 'When they respond it is really satisfying. Some of them don't respond at all. There was one bloke down there, he didn't talk to anyone, he just kept grunting. We were playing with him and talking to him and he started laughing. And the nurse said "That's the first time I've ever seen him actually respond." And it was really satisfying to think that we'd helped him, and, at the same time, we'd achieved something.'

And the next speaker also worked in a mental hospital, both before and after his release from a nearby Borstal:

> 'I really think I've done well. I've done something with my life. Instead of staying there in Borstal, just doing nothing, I've gained something out of life, it's pulled me out of that situation.'

Young people need the chance to find roles which give them that kind of satisfaction and that kind of self-respect. We may call the experience which gives them that chance 'work' or 'community service', it doesn't really matter. In Eastern Europe young people run their own railway line, in Britain and in the United States they run emergency rescue services. A programme in a New York hospital shows that work, community service, work and careers experience, can be combined in an imaginative — and much needed — programme of youth involvement. The organiser of this programme said: 'They are not voyeurs, they are contributors' — and they work on emergency wards and in the operating theatre itself.

We talked earlier of the present separation of childhood and youth and the need to blur this separation. It is simple to give young people a role. It means admitting them to our world in ways and through means that are in accordance with their needs and potential. It is not asking a lot to demand that they have those roles from the age of 13 onwards. After all, it is to play these roles, within their family or within the community, that many young people are escaping from school at present.

Reality

Finally there is reality, which hardly needs explaining. It means doing, learning, enjoying, participating at first hand. It means that some things are better learned about than taught; some are better experienced than advised upon; some things are better found than given.

The apprentice situation which had one experienced worker and one young person learning from him is fast disappearing. Young apprentices these days are taught in classes. A girl in one of them told us why it didn't work for her:

'I think you learn better by doing it. Like electricity: I reckon we'd learn more if we was doing it than sitting there, learning the signs. If we had a bloke going round fitting these houses out and we went round with him. That would be good. If you see what the bloke's doing you learn more than you do on a diagram. What we do now — he tells you to do something and if it's wrong he'll say, "That's not right — do it again".'

And an instructor in a class for the young unemployed told us about another kind of unreality:

'The early part of the decorating course is spent working on boards in the decorating room, putting up paper, scraping it off and trying again. The first time they do it they're quite proud of it, but when they have to scrape it off and start again, they get bored very quickly. You have to find them something to do which has some use. What we are doing here is still a bit of a game, to some extent.'

Games are for children. If we want children to grow up, then the games have got to stop. But the catch is always the question: 'They won't be able to cope, will they? The real world will be too much for them, won't it?'

Perhaps we should raise our expectations of the young a little higher. In earlier chapters we quoted a young man who was working in a scrap-metal yard. He talked about his first day, about the man who employed him, about the way he had been expected to break up a car:

'Then I just chopped it straight through the middle. He says, "That's good, that is." I was right glad. After I'd finished he said "Want a drink?" So I went for a drink with him that night, although I'm under age.'

13 An Alternative Future

It is fashionable to see youth unemployment as the problem.
Presently we have remedial 'special programmes'. The next
'solution' in vogue is an all-purpose institution for 16 to 18 year-
olds, which offers incentives to young people to keep them off the
streets and out of the statistics. Pressure groups and youth
organisations, politicians and local authorities show signs of a
disturbing unity of purpose.

But the phenomenon derives from a far older problem, in
modern welfare, wealth-producing economies: 'What do we do
with youth?' Young people understand unemployment very well,
they spend most of the first two decades of life learning about it, to
their cost and ours. Many young people recognise that this is a
waste, and so do many parents and people involved in the public
services which look after young people.

When there was no problem of youth unemployment, the wider
issue could be, and was, easily overlooked. Everything seemed to
turn out all right in the end. Young people got jobs, became adults.
Now many of them don't and can't, and that is our fault. It will be
our fault too, if we cover up the failings in our attitudes to young
people, and our ways of dealing with them, both pre- and post-16,
with a new 'buffer-zone' which leaves everything that happens to
young people, before and after, just the same.

We have talked about the need for incorporating '3 R's' of a new
kind into education, and the need to make opportunities available
from 13 years onwards, so that young people can leave the
educational mainstream for a period which suits them. There have
been other changes implied in the descriptions of provision for
youth in preceding chapters, and now it is time to make these
explicit. These suggestions are workable, and they are no more
expensive than current expenditure in the 'youth' field, especially if
we count the hidden costs of dealing with the problems that this
current expenditure *creates*.

Not all these suggestions are based on what young people have
said to us. They have given us clear evidence of dissatisfaction with
many aspects of the present system of education, advice, experience

and growing up, and they have also told us about things which work, for them. Some young people have found that academic courses, youth clubs and professional advice and counselling work for them. Any programme of action should, for their sake, contain these elements; but in their proper place and context. At present they constitute the policy, and the policy rules.

When other styles and methods find a place, they cut through 'the policy' with refreshing ease. The MSC programmes are a good example. New styles, new methods and, above all, new *people* have a chance to make a contribution. The potential may be in danger of submersion by inexperience and cautiousness of officials, it may be drawn to a super 16-18 institution and away from more fully developing popular involvement. But when it has worked as a vehicle for popular involvement, it has really worked for young people.

Alternatives to present policies and systems do not do well. They have little money and they are condemned in the press:

'PARENTS BLAMED FOR MISLEADING CHILDREN ON CAREER CHOICES.

Out of date advice from parents is harming the career prospects of many of Britain's school leavers, says a report being prepared for the EEC. It calls for earlier careers advice in schools to offset this . . .'   *(Times Educational Supplement,* November 1978)

This is an example of "more of the same". An alternative conclusion would be to call for parents to be more a part of the network, professional and lay, institutional and individual and collective, which offers advice and help to the young. Because if young people are taking notice of their *parents* — and this report says they are — and if they are not taking much of careers teachers — and our conversations suggest they aren't . . . surely one of the things that must happen is that parents are better serviced with information, and that their advice, poorly informed as it may be, is recognised as being listened to by many young people? The system has reduced these parents to the status of mere 'onlookers', blamed by the professionals for making a mess of things.

So we propose alternatives. Not *an alternative* to what is going on, but different ways of doing things, operating side by side. The needs of individual young people, and the environments in which they can best flourish and grow up, will always vary. The programmes for the young unemployed are the only major part of present provision which pay any recognition to that and offer, in theory at least, a variety of chances.

Alternatives mean choice — real choice, not the spurious variety which pervades debates about education, where the only difference between two 'choices' is whether you pay (or are able to pay) or not. Or that other choice, between staying in or dropping out. Real choice only exists between fundamentally different ways of doing things. There are three important ingredients in any public service system which, mixed in differing proportions, could produce a variety of ways of doing things: institutional action, collective action, individual action. That means having it provided for you, doing it together, being self-reliant. There are other ingredients, like what is offered, how big your 'network' (that applies to all three ways of doing things) and how it is controlled and directed. Unless we have alternatives, different ways of doing things, how will we learn? There are many people who find the present system of public services, relying as it does on one response, and that an institutional one, to be oppressive.

Alternatives are needed in education, alternatives are needed in work, and alternatives are needed in that grey area of formal and informal advice. Alternatives are needed in leisure and recreational activities. Alternatives to institutions: opportunities to explore various ways of meeting the needs of individual young people and blurring the boundaries between provider, client and onlooker. Alternatives mean opportunities to turn two million unemployed people and many millions of under or uselessly employed people, including the young, into a resource, rather than leaving them as a "problem", or treating them as "clients".

We will begin with some alternatives for education. It's tempting to start with 'Local education authorities should . . .' but that assumes that local education authorities are necessary. Instead, why not remove education from its position as a party political bone of contention, and make it merely a political one, so that its priorities and policies are decided in a wider arena than that delineated by Party stances and professional interests? It would not be inconceivable to apply the 'pot of gold' principle pioneered by the MSC special programmes to education and other public services as well as to services for the unemployed. Since 65-70 per cent of educational resources come from the exchequer via the Rate Support Grant, with the rest coming from local taxation through rates, it should be possible to lay down criteria centrally which provide a broad framework within which local political debate and plans for action could emerge, which would represent the request for a share of the "pot of gold". To change the metaphor, central resources would act as a carrot, attracting the areas towards two goals, which would be embodied in the criteria: a variety of approaches, and popular participation, both in planning and delivery. Such a proposal would weaken the grip of the local authorities, and strengthen the hold that the public as a whole has on its servants, by making central government resource-giving bodies function as *enablers* rather than givers and controllers merely. That is proper devolution.

The MSC hesitated to take its own 'pot of gold' arrangements to this logical conclusion. (The idea of sponsorship would have died quickly if the funds for programmes for the unemployed had been channelled through the Rate Support Grant). But the wrong substitute was chosen. These were the thirty or so large areas, between which the pot of gold was divided according to need. Each area was delegated a considerable amount of power, but this was held by high level bureaucrats at the committee level, and inexperienced civil servants at the official level. So local, lay, public involvement was allowed only to the extent of sponsorship. A shame that the chance to get people together at that level, using the money as a carrot, was missed.

What kind of variety should we be looking for? There is plenty written elsewhere about alternative education, and here we only have room to sketch ideas which, if resources were not already consumed by the 'policy', could be put into practice right away.

Crises have provoked some of these. A school in a Cambridgeshire village was closed by the local education authority. Parents took it over and eventually bought it. That meant collective action and collective involvement. It's sad that it has become a private school, but at least it is theirs, they can be involved in it, and they are. Two choices are demonstrated by this example: some people like, and flourish best, in small environments. We're tempted to say *many* people, indeed. Writing about small-scale technology, E.F. Schumacher said:

> '. . . we need methods and equipment that are cheap enough so that they are accessible to virtually everyone; suitable for small-scale application; and compatible with man's need for creativity.' *(Small is Beautiful)*.

That thought applies to education, as well as other public services.

The second choice this example demonstrates is that open to the parent, who can now be a participant-parent rather than an onlooker-parent. This is clearly easier for middle-class parents, but it would be directly transferable to anywhere, if the penalty of having to buy the wretched school was removed and if 'professional' barriers were removed. It isn't just that 500 village primary schools have been closed by local authorities in the past ten years. The issue is wider than that. Those who want it should be able to choose a small environment, and parental involvement would not be there simply as a way to make ends meet. Some people want to be so involved, many more are not just onlookers — they may be the' unemployed — why waste them?

The collective approach should not be confined to parents. Many young people say that it should not be. Say what you like about school, it does get you away from parents for a bit. We have referred to one alternative approach, using volunteers and students, in Bristol. Here is an example of the involvement of local people in Gratiot County, Michigan:

'In May 1974, the Mid Michigan Community Action Council began to develop an organised network of community volunteers to provide first-hand information to students on careers and the working world. The Council's effort has expanded to include approximately 730 volunteers county wide and is still growing. Volunteers participate as classroom speakers, mock job interviewers . . . All activities . . . are available to the six Gratiot County school districts. Activities are accessible to local teachers/schools through the Council's Dial-a-Speaker telephone service, which matches the need of the student group to the volunteer resources. available . . .' *(The Work Education Consortium, An Inventory of Projects in Progress*, National Manpower Institute, Washington 1978).

Learning exchanges, 'people's yellow pages', volunteer-tutoring programmes and apprentice-learning systems: all these approaches are based on the idea that there is value in involving people other than professionals in the education process. It is alarming to see how poorly these necessary complements to institutional and professional educational services have been developed. Collective involvement should not solely apply to 'careers and the working world', it should reach more widely. Young people must be brought into direct, first-hand contact with that working world and, as important, with all the processes and people at work in society and local communities. Many of these people have potential and abilities which reach far beyond their 'station' and work-role. Many of them find their 'station' and work-role unsatisfying and undignified. The school caretaker, the postman that young people meet, may have better qualifications and experience to be 'teachers' than the professional. We know that, because we have met them, and they have taught us.

Part of any 'collective' response must be young people themselves. In 'On Location' and in many other contexts, we have seen young people working with one another, teaching others and making decisions. In Northern Ireland they are taking action as well as decisions in sensitively organised programmes for the unemployed, as well as participating in the para-military organisations. In both contexts the lesson is the same: involve us, young people are saying. There is a difference between the belated recognition of this by educationists operating unemployment schemes, and the blatant manipulation of it by political extremists. The National Front know how to exploit the desire of young people and others for a voice and a role, too. We ought to be smart enough to heed their lesson, which recognises the need for *risk* as well as role.

Touring a lavishly equipped polytechnic, we saw the resources which back up a long established tradition of *individual* action in tertiary education. We said 'Amazing' as our inbred distaste for technology made us flinch at the sight of note-takers in earphones sitting in individual booths and watching cassette-loaded video television screens. Education technology always looks like second-hand learning moved to third-hand and beyond. But those silent individuals had the choice to learn in *that* way open to them. Why should younger people not have similar chances and choices? Not just to fill up free periods, but to decide and negotiate other ways of learning. And why cannot individuals go out and fix up their own learning experiences, with the cobbler, the butcher, the bank, the farmer? And why can't they say 'I want to learn from you', even if 'you' is simply a person who has made a video-tape about their work, and this is available to the young person. Why not?

The reason 'why not' is that there is insufficient flexibility in our education system, except at the margins, to allow for this. This is because we have, especially at the secondary level, subjects, rather than courses. As one progresses into further, higher and adult education, courses become more common. In secondary education in other countries students often have courses rather than subjects open to them. It seems that this is sensible in terms of the flexibility it can offer, and that it is appropriate to the capabilities of both adults and young people.

There is another angle. Why close schools for long periods every year? There is a lot to be said for keeping institutions open for 48 weeks a year, and dividing that year into 4, twelve-week cycles, during which 12-week, or '12-week multiple' courses can take place. This not only makes better use of the plant itself, but it removes much of the inflexibility of present practices. You cannot mix earning and learning, for example, if the institutional part of your learning is closed down for long periods. Not long ago we would have said that longer opening would change the state of affairs whereby professional teachers are well-paid for a 36 week, 5-hour day working year. (The teachers themselves admitted that these are their working hours by their 'withdrawal of goodwill' industrial action in April 1979.) Now we are inclined to see this as a good kind of work-load, with teachers in the vanguard of shorter working hours. Much of the void this will create in longer opening could be filled by the non-professionally certificated workers. And they would help to fill the void in education *outside* the institutions also.

From the secondary level onwards, schools should work on the same timetable as a normal working day, with four hours in the morning (say 2, two hour sessions) and four hours in the afternoon. This would provide four sessions a day, instead of six, seven or eight periods. There could then be a fifth, evening session. This all sounds a bit laborious, but we have spelled it out, because if educational institutions operated in this way, it would be far easier to organise your own involvement, as an individual, in the process, in a way which would suit your own needs.

School timetables are often very complicated. During a visit to a school in the United States, we were at first hopelessly confused by the range of 'courses', some compulsory, some 'core' and some elective. These last were increasingly available to students as they grew up. 'How is the timetable worked out?' we asked, expecting to be shown a room full of deputy-heads and computers. The answer was simple — every day looked just the same. That may have been oversimple, but to say that a course system will prove too complex to organise is to make excuses. We have tried to imagine what the system we are proposing would look like to an individual.

Firstly, let us base the thinking on the premises that after eleven years of age, each of us has an entitlement to seven years worth of education. Not just institutional education. This education would be partly composed of a 'core' and partly of a chosen 'elective' area. We shall not discuss what these two parts should contain, except to say that we would have '3 R's' in the core, and they would be *our* '3 R's'. In structural terms, this education would mean, for each year of entitlement, three (out of the four) 12-week cycles, where each week is made up of 5 days, each day contains 4 sessions. So the total individual entitlement is, in session terms, 720 sessions per year. Over seven years this would mean 5000 sessions. So the individual has 5000 education credits, allowances . . . vouchers?

You can spend these at any time in your life. You can negotiate with a proportion of them at any one time, and cash them in for other educational purposes, travel for example. If you want more, you can buy them, or they may be awarded by way of grant or benefit.

Here is a fifteen-year-old, thinking about the beginning of a forthcoming 12-week cycle (240 sessions). With the help of advisors — parents, friends, others — he decides that he wants to use only two-thirds of these, and keep the others for later years. So he has 160 sessions. He plans to spend 13 sessions a week on education, and the rest of the time — a day and a half or so — to work. Of the education, he decides to take 2 sessions each day learning, as an apprentice, in a garage. The educational credit for those sessions goes to the garage, who cashes it in. Since our lad is contributing while he's there, they pay him a little back. It's not a wage, more a token. If he chose rather to *work* then he would get paid a *wage* for it. He chooses to spend some of the rest of his educational time in a programme-learning centre. Some of the rest he spends with teachers. He has chosen courses in Applied Maths (mechanics) and Elementary Chemistry (for strict beginners). Some of this time is spent in a study group which discusses political issues, with help from non-professional 'teachers'. The 'core' takes up much of the rest of his time. The time that he has chosen to spend in institutional education is spent in a small, local building. He has chosen this because it suits him, but there are other bases, of different sizes, which he could have chosen. The programme-learning centre is elsewhere, as are other facilities for specialised work.

Such a system could apply to the 51-year-old as well as to the 15-year-old. Why shouldn't adults have part-day-release, or full-day-release, or several day-release to go and learn, or to do something else? Especially when the work they do is undemanding and boring? Here the 12-week cycle also applies. And if the job which is being left undone by such a person is vital, perhaps a younger person, seeking work or apprentice-learning, will be able to fill it? It's time we recognised the possibility of work-sharing.

There are, and should be, a variety of ways on which a system like this could work. It could be a glorified version of those famous "enrolment days" which adult education thrives on. Queues of people, all round the gym, waiting to sign on for French Conversation (advanced). But it would be more than a question of simply 'signing on'. Many young people may want help and advice, and they'll be trying to fix up more than classes. They'll want to get study groups together, and fix up apprentice-learning and work at the same time. And they'll want to decide what style of school they want for their institution-based learning.

What is needed to make it work is an imaginative alliance of modern technology, communication mechanisms (print, phone, video) and people. This must be imaginative enough to break through and break up the present fragmented and professionally defined services that are available, and re-shape them. What they offer must be a response to the needs of individuals, rather than to the needs of adults to keep young people as children; of professional teachers to operate second-hand, academic study, and of colleges to serve the local labour-market.

Of course, our fifteen-year-old (who has now changed sex, in the interests of fairness) may not get everything she had hoped from the 12-week cycle: her use of the technological, communication and people networks may lead her to the conclusion that, for example, she can only take her chemistry course in the evening, because the day-time course clashes with the day on which she could be at the garage. So she may switch things round, taking a different course, or looking at the one-to-one tutoring she could get locally from yellow pages, or on the Ceefax screen. She may see something there that interests her — elementary guitar, say. Or, sitting down for a chat with a friendly advisor — at her own request — she may discuss whether it might be best to spend the next twelve weeks between apprentice-learning at the garage and other work, with no courses at all.

These are just the bones of a suggestion which shows how the institutional diet can be leavened and varied, how work and education can be mixed, how people other than those with professional qualifications can and must be involved.

In the area of work we have already noted how the self-interests of employer and worker, professional and politician, are detrimental to the dignity and prospects of young people, whether in the field of work or community service. It is the early school-leaver who is at the greatest disadvantage here. Equal opportunities legislation does not help the young, and employment protection has hindered them.

We would make five proposals. The first would be investment in agencies which we would call 'enabling agencies'. These would seek to match young people to work in a variety of settings. Where necessary these agencies would act as brokers in the matching process, to overcome exploitation of young people, both financially and in terms of their dignity.

Secondly, there should be positive encouragement for the involvement of young people and adults in the personal public 'community services'. There should be funds available for those services to pay people who are involved in them. The anachronistic association between 'voluntary' work and 'unpaid' work should end as should the pretence that in all work that the young undertake they should necessarily be trainees. People who 'volunteer' for public service involvement should be *offered* payment. It would then be open to *them* to refuse, or reduce it, as they wish.

Thirdly, there is a need for a 'bank' to enable the development of youth enterprises. The present training workshop provision of the MSC confuses training with 'enterprise' in the sense of making and selling. This is one direction for industrial investment in the future, and it would encourage small-scale enterprises.

Fourthly, we need to extend the idea of sponsorship and community initiative to other public services, to break the stranglehold of professionals and institutions.

Finally, it seems there must be legislation to prevent discrimination by professionals against 'lay' volunteers, and by adults against young people. We mistrust legislation, but it seems more and more necessary.

Our poor youth action organisations, with the less poor MSC-funded community service schemes, would form an obvious base for the first proposal. They could be funded by stopping all central and local government grants to 'provision for children' organisations and services, which should become commercial if they wish to continue. Existing careers and counselling services should be taken over by these agencies and stripped of their professional tendencies. You cannot divorce advice about work from work itself, and that is why so many young people listen to their parents, however ill-informed they may be. These agencies should be as varied and participative in their practices as we have recommended educationists to be.

Our second proposal would rid voluntarism of its 'philanthropic/

sacrifice' and hence middle-class aura. It means that increased public spending in the welfare services would not merely be job creation for professionals, but would change the composition of these services. They would be less expert, more labour-intensive, *genuinely* taking up the slack created by technological change in the industrial sector, and providing the satisfaction industrial work alone already lacks.

The extension of alternatives in other public services is happening in some areas. Housing, for example, or city partnerships. Certainly our present ability to finance alternatives is insufficient. (The Report of the Wolfenden Committee on Voluntary Organisations missed almost every possible point and potential for development.) Certainly, too, most voluntary organisations, in many public service fields, are happy to ape the policy, and play on the fringe of the system. None of this will do.

This amounts to a need for a cultural revolution, rather than a super-institution or a great debate. With it, we can create a *continuous* system of 'learning and earning' and do away with existing institutions, programmes and services. With it, we can end the situation we have described which exists in so many of our services, where the policy only suits some people, some of the time, and have, through the range of opportunities (in terms of what they are *and* how they are operated) a system which can suit all the people, all the time. There is enormous potential to develop these new styles and approaches to education and work, to learning and doing, to role and responsibility, to participation and dignity, through co-operative approaches at a local level. We will not find answers to the problems of growing up by creating a super-Ministry of Education Work Experience and Training. All our experience suggests that government needs breaking down rather than rationalising into bigger corporate units. It is at the local level that coherence is needed, and a coherence which must be less exclusive and less remote rather than more so. It can be done. There is a wealth of talent and ability at the community level, and an understanding of the community development processes which would be a necessary preamble to local planning, the request for funds, the operation of the kind of integrated education-work networks we have outlined. Most of the problems of community workers at present stem from 'the system' rather than the lack of ability and potential among the public. We also have, as a result of the MSC programmes in particular, a growing number of entrepreneurs, animateurs, catalysts, call them what you like, who have the skills needed to pioneer and develop new ways of working with young people rather than providing for them. We have many professionals who are disillusioned with the way they have to work at present. Finally there are practices to observe elsewhere, and that have developed here: Education-Work Councils in the United States, local groups working to overcome the difficulties of sponsor-fragmentation in our own programmes for the unemployed; community councils, self-help groups and individuals committed to the regeneration of community life and the control of people over the affairs which govern their lives.

All this exists. What we need now is an act of will, a recognition that it is time we met our needs through the potential, ability and energy of people, rather than the requirements and restraints of institutions. Because if we do not revolutionise our attitudes to young people, and our ways of dealing with them, we will be in dire trouble.